MACBETH

WILLIAM SHAKESPEARE

Edited by Jeannie Heppell
Head of English, Queen Margaret's School, Escrick, York
Associate Editor Ann Green, M.A., M. Litt., Oxon.

Henderson Study System devised by Jeannie Heppell
© Celandine International 1995

HOW TO USE THIS TEXT

On the next page you will find a list of major themes contained in this text. They are in different colours. By following the instructions below, you will form a coding system which will give you immediate access to the material you will need to study the themes.

At the back of the text you will find sheets of stickers. These correspond with coloured markers at the right-hand edge of the pages. Peel off the sticker and place it exactly in position, over the matching colour guide. Fold the tab along the half-colour line, and stick down the white half to the back of the page. This allows matching colour tabs to protrude over the edge of the pages, all in line, throughout your book, making it easy to locate the material to study your theme. The references you will need for the theme will be underlined in the appropriate colour on the pages of text.

You will find that:

• **THEMES ARE <u>HIGHLIGHTED</u>**

• **QUOTATIONS ARE IMMEDIATELY ACCESSIBLE**

• **YOU HAVE INSTANT RECOGNITION OF DOMINANT THEMES**

• **YOU CAN SEE AT A GLANCE THE DOMINANT IMAGES**

• **MATERIAL FOR ESSAYS IS READILY AVAILABLE FOR YOU TO RESPOND TO INDIVIDUALLY, AVOIDING PREPARED PLANS**

• **YOUR REVISION IS ALREADY STRUCTURED**

N.B. The numbering on this text is actual, overriding split-verse lines.

MAJOR THEMES IN THIS TEXT

DECEPTION

IMAGES OF EVIL

FEAR

COURAGE

KINGSHIP AND THE CROWN

IRONY

AMBITION

GUILT AND BLOOD

JUSTICE AND NATURAL ORDER

TREACHERY

DAMNATION AND HELL

CHILDREN

MACBETH: THE THEMES

A glance at your colour-coded volume will immediately show that not all the themes run throughout the play. **Ambition** is concentrated at the start, **fear** occurs in clusters in the centre, whilst **justice and natural order** moves to a focus towards the end of the drama. Nevertheless, these ideas are important. **Ambition** is the motive which provokes Macbeth into taking the witches' prophecies as indications of reality; he wants what they appear to offer. His ambition, fostered by his wife's will, and by her ambition for him, is stronger than his moral vision. So ambition initiates Macbeth's step into crime and confusion. Subsequently, **fear** takes over as a spur to action: fear of the imagined deed, of his wife's scorn, of the consequences of murder; then, after the deed, of discovery through Banquo or Macduff, and of failure to secure the crown for his possible heirs. The powers of darkness understand and play on his fears but also create for him a sense of false confidence in his safety, so that the fear theme is ousted by courage again in the final act. The **justice and order** theme is seen in Act 1, with the sense of the order and ritual of Duncan's court, which is quickly threatened and destroyed by his murder. Macbeth fears human justice and divine retribution, but once the murder is enacted, moves into a world increasingly prey to disorder and his own injustices. In the final act a sense of reviving order, and a movement towards justice, often expressed in imagery of healing, are seen. Malcolm ends the drama by restoring in his kingship the order lost to Scotland since the murder of his father violated the natural code.

Of the themes which run throughout, the **kingship** theme, with its symbol the crown, links closely with that of **justice and natural order**, for these are qualities for which the virtuous king stands. Macbeth covets the power and respect that accompanies kingship, and he desires it for his heirs, hence the force of the apparition which shows him a line of 'gold-bound brows' descended from Banquo. Yet when he gains the crown, he forfeits all the qualities for which he coveted it, except its power, which he uses destructively. He becomes not king, but tyrant, a term used repeatedly of him in the last two acts of the play. Act Five introduces images of true kingship in England's Edward the Confessor, the holy king, and in the young heir, Malcolm. As the two images of tyrant and virtuous king stand side by side, we see what, ironically, Macbeth has lost.

Two themes are colour-coded which need little comment: **treachery** and **hell and damnation**. Our attention is directed to them from the beginning of the action. As treachery proliferates after the initial example of the Thane of Cawdor, things reach the point where Macduff's treachery to his wrongful king, Macbeth, is equated with loyalty towards the true heir, Malcolm.

Hell and damnation is a theme which covers all manifestations of the supernatural, but has only been colour-coded outside the main witch scenes, since these are self-evident. Shakespeare's dramatic focus centres not so much on the Witches themselves and their apparent foreknowledge, as on Macbeth's response to their prophecies, and the way in which his decisions (aided by Lady Macbeth in the first place) determine his downfall and fulfil the prophecies.

The theme of **children** needs some explanation, since it is often present not so much in words as in visual images and in dramatic situations. The father and child pairs of Banquo and Fleance, Siward and his son, Macduff and his children, each set up for us the notions of generation bonding and of natural inheritance. They underline the fact that Macbeth, despite the reference of his wife to having given suck, appears to have no children, and yet is obsessed with horror at the idea of passing the crown to another man's son. That two of the apparitions take the form of children, one a bloody child, the other a child with a crown, is perhaps a reading by the Witches of Macbeth's subconscious obsession. Certainly, Macbeth's killing of Macduff's son is meant to convey the extremes of brutality and unnaturalness; it is interesting that earlier in the play it is prefigured by Lady Macbeth's threat that she would have killed her own child at the breast rather than be a coward like her husband.

The most prevalent themes of the play are **deception** or false-seeming, and **images of evil**. These combine to give us a horrifying picture of man's vulnerability to evil, and a sense of swift and inevitable destruction for him who has turned to it. Evil works through deception; the devil is the father of lies. The Witches first confuse, then deceive Macbeth. He and his wife deceive Duncan and the court with their hypocritical display of loyal respect. Macbeth deceives the hired murderers into thinking Banquo to be their oppressor. Even the virtuous are driven by the prevailing distrust into using deception, as Malcolm does when he tests Macduff's integrity by his pretence of unkingly vices. The Witches' apparitions deceptively suggest security to Macbeth as he misinterprets their ambiguity - only when it is too late does he realise that he has been "paltered with in a double sense" by the powers of evil. The main images that accompany the idea of deception are the flower, smiles and assumed robes which hide the reality of serpents, daggers, and distorted shrunken shape.

So, Macbeth is taken in by the evil that looks like good, and his own crime causes an increasing chaos in the world around him: darkness and disorder where there should be light and order. These are both the results of evil and the conditions in which it operates. So Macbeth needs darkness to conceal his villainous actions (I, iv, 57-58), and Lady Macbeth summons darkness when she invokes evil (I, v, 41-55). Unnatural portents accompany the murder of Duncan: his horses eat each other, and a lowly owl kills a falcon. The unnatural and bestial ingredients of the Witches' brew show a similar perversion, and Macbeth himself hails the hags as creators of chaos (IV, i, 49-62). We see disorder in the tormented mind of Lady Macbeth, within the family of Macduff, within the suffering society of Scotland. All these have grown by relentless logic from Macbeth's original murder of the king. To the Elizabethan mind, sin caused a disruption in the natural order and harmony of man, society and the cosmos, which recalls original chaos; the sin of killing the king and usurping the throne was an extreme which mirrored Satan's rebellion against God.

Two themes which contribute strongly to the tragic feeling of the play are those of **guilt**, with its imagery of blood, and **courage**. As a tragic hero, even though he is also villain, Macbeth does demand our pity, never more than when he is traumatised by guilt after the murder of Duncan, or in the banquet scene. He cannot say "Amen", he sees himself as the killer of sleep; he sees, but cannot touch the "air-drawn dagger"; he quails in the glare of the "blood-boltered Banquo". The images of blood that fill the play are symbolic of his guilt, and of Lady Macbeth's stifled conscience which recreates in her sleep the horror of Duncan's blood and the eternal blood-stains on her hand. They may be "butcher" and "fiend-like queen", but we pity them as we see them destroyed by depraved actions which have not, ironically, removed from them a subconscious perception of their own sin.

Then, **courage**. Our introduction to Macbeth is his valiant single combat with the rebel Macdonwald. His courage is a soldier's virtue; manly, violent, used in the service of his King, and justly rewarded by him. The next focus is revealing: his wife taunts Macbeth with lack of courage in the face of murder, and so deeply does he care to be rejected by her for cowardice and effeminacy ("Such I account thy love"), that he steels himself to overcome his qualms and

proves himself "a man again". Yet he recognises that his crime has taken him past manhood into bestiality ("who dares do more is none"). The pattern of terror and recovery in response to his wife's scorn is repeated in the scene with Banquo's ghost, but the violence of his emotions now drives him to desperate recourse to the Witches. They, too, understand and play on his need for courage; the apparitions give him a sense of false security, and the result is an uncontrollable bravado. Buoyed up by an illusion of manly action, he takes revenge on Macduff, and sinks to his lowest point: the pointless slaughter of an innocent child. It would seem that he is beyond respect. Yet in the last scenes he regains something of his original bravery. Faced with a world without meaning which he recognises that he has himself created, his heady courage takes him outside the safety of the castle, where he meets Macduff in single combat, and so the last prophecy can be fulfilled. Even as he boasts that he "bears a charmed life", his last assurance is taken from him: Macduff was not born of woman. He summons up his courage, and is killed, like Siward's son, with his wounds on the front - a soldier's death. The wheel has come full circle.

So what of **irony**? You may find this the hardest of the themes to deal with, but it is the most vital for an understanding of the nature of the play. It takes many forms.

The structural irony of the drama and the intensity with which we react to it, are provided by our clear knowledge throughout that the Witches are evil, that Macbeth's actions are depraved, and that every step he thinks he takes to save himself, is actually a step towards damnation. Because Macbeth does not share this conscious understanding, lesser ironies multiply. Macbeth makes comments on his own position which we know to be false; other characters on stage voice opinions which are contradicted by our fuller knowledge; or the whole situation is ironic, like Macbeth's last visit to the Witches, which despite his illusions, can only worsen things for him. We can be shown contradictory things simultaneously, as when Malcolm orders his troops to "shadow their numbers" with the branches of trees, even as Macbeth is exulting that he cannot be beaten until "Birnam wood remove to Dunsinane".

Shakespeare's plays are rich both in themes and the images that express them; each subsequent reading tends to bring another aspect to light. If these few selections have helped you to understand the play, so that you can return to it and make your own additions, and capture a sense of excitement in the process, then this edition has fulfilled its purpose.

Ann Green, M.A., M. Litt., Oxon.

ABOUT JEANNIE HEPPELL

Jeannie Heppell is an Honours graduate of Nottingham University. She has been Head of English at Queen Margaret's School, Escrick Park, for the past twelve years and was formerly an 'A' level examiner for the Oxford Board. Previous to this, she was Deputy Director of Theatre at Ampleforth College where she devised a version of this system in order to have swift access to specific areas of play scripts. The system adapted well to the preparation of texts for examination and has been used with outstanding success by her students for over a decade at both Advanced and GCSE levels. She lives in Yorkshire with her husband and is particularly fond of West Highland terriers.

MACBETH

CHARACTERS

DUNCAN, *King of Scotland*

MALCOLM
DONALBAIN } *his sons*

MACBETH
BANQUO } *Generals of the King's Army*

MACDUFF
LENNOX
ROSS
MENTEITH } *Noblemen of Scotland*
ANGUS
CAITHNESS

FLEANCE, *son to* BANQUO

SIWARD, *Earl of Northumberland, General of the English Forces*

YOUNG SIWARD, *his son*

SEYTON, *an Officer attending on* MACBETH

BOY, *son to* MACDUFF

An ENGLISH DOCTOR, *a* SCOTCH DOCTOR, *a* SOLDIER, *a* PORTER, *an* OLD MAN

LADY MACBETH

LADY MACDUFF

GENTLEWOMAN *attending on* LADY MACBETH

HECATE, *and three* WITCHES

LORDS, GENTLEMEN, OFFICERS, SOLDIERS, MURDERERS, ATTENDANTS, MESSENGERS

The **Ghost of** BANQUO, *and several other* APPARITIONS

SCENE – *In the end of the Fourth Act, in* ENGLAND;
through the rest of the Play,
in SCOTLAND; *and chiefly at* MACBETH'S *Castle.*

ACT ONE, SCENE ONE
AN OPEN PLACE, *Thunder and Lightning*

Enter three WITCHES.

1 WITCH When shall we three meet again
    In thunder, lightening, or in rain?
2 WITCH When the *(1)* hurlyburly's done,
    When the battle's lost and won.
3 WITCH That will be ere the set of sun.   **5**
1 WITCH Where the place?
2 WITCH Upon the heath.
3 WITCH There to *(2)* meet with Macbeth.
1 WITCH I come, *(3)* Graymalkin!
ALL Paddock calls: – anon, –   **10**
    (4) Fair is foul, and foul is fair:
    Hover through the fog and filthy air.

                (WITCHES *vanish.*

ACT ONE, SCENE TWO
A CAMP NEAR FORRES

Alarum within. Enter KING DUNCAN, MALCOLM, DONALBAIN, LENNOX,
with Attendants, *meeting a bleeding* Soldier.

DUNCAN What bloody man is that? He can report,
    As seemeth by his plight, *(5)* of the revolt
    The newest state.
MALCOLM   This is the sergeant,
    Who, like a good and *(6)* hardy soldier, fought   **5**
    'Gainst my captivity. – Hail, brave friend!
    Say to the king the knowledge of the *(7)* broil,
    As thou didst leave it.
SOLDIER   *(8)* Doubtful it stood;
    As two spent swimmers that do cling together   **10**
    And choke their art. The merciless Macdonwald, –
    Worthy to be a rebel – for to that

1 uproar, tumult of battle

2 Clearly Macbeth is the target of the three Witches. Evil is thus instigated by the supernatural powers, but it is left to Macbeth's will whether he acts on the prophecies or not.

3 Graymalkin and Paddock are names for witches' 'familiars', cat and toad respectively.

4 The first of many images of confusion and inversion, which reflect the moral uncertainty connected with the Witches and spread by Macbeth's murder of Duncan.

5 the most recent happenings in the rebellion

6 brave

7 skirmish

8 The battle was undecided, like the movements of two weary swimmers whose clinging together impedes their progress.

The (1) multiplying villainies of nature   **15**
Do swarm upon him, – from the Western isles
Of (2) kerns and gallowglasses is supplied;
And (3) fortune, on his damned quarrel smiling,
Show'd like a rebel's whore. But all's too weak:
For brave Macbeth, – well he deserves that name –   **20**
Disdaining fortune, with his brandish'd steel,
Which (4) smok'd with bloody execution,
Like (5) valour's minion,
Carv'd out his passage till he fac'd the slave;
And ne'er shook hands, nor bade farewell to him,   **25**
Till he (6) unseam'd him from the nave to the chaps,
And fix'd his head upon our battlements.

DUNCAN O valiant cousin! worthy gentleman!

SOLDIER As whence the sun 'gins his reflection
Shipwrecking storms and direful thunders break;   **30**
So (7) from that spring, whence comfort seem'd to come,
Discomfort swells. Mark, King of Scotland, mark;
No sooner justice had, with valour arm'd,
Compell'd these skipping kerns (8) to trust their heels,
But the Norweyan lord, (9) surveying vantage,   **35**
With (10) furbish'd arms and new supplies of men,
Began a fresh assault.

DUNCAN   Dismay'd not this
Our captains, Macbeth and Banquo?

SOLDIER   Yes;   **40**
As (11) sparrows eagles, or the hare the lion.
If I say (12) sooth, I must report they were
As cannons (13) overcharg'd with double cracks;
So they
Doubly redoubled strokes upon the foe: **45**
(14) Except they meant to bathe in reeking wounds,
Or memorise another Golgotha,
I cannot tell . . .
But I am faint; my gashes cry for help.

DUNCAN So well (15) thy words become thee as thy wounds;   **50**
They smack of honour both. – Go, get him surgeons.
                              Exit Soldier, *attended.*
Who comes here?

MALCOLM   The worthy Thane of Ross.

LENNOX (16) What a haste looks through his eyes! So should he look
That seems to speak things strange.   **55**

Marginal glosses:

1 because of the way that evil qualities breed in him

2 foot and mounted troops from Ireland

3 Good luck, favouring the rebel, followed him like a cheap prostitute

4 steamed with the blood of his slaughter

5 the darling of Courage

6 slit him up the middle from belly to jaw

7 Disaster comes often from the very source that promised hope, just as thunder-storms rise in the East where we look for sunshine.
An ironic comment, more true than Duncan or the soldier realises, since Duncan relies heavily on Macbeth, who will so soon be his murderer.

8 to take to their heels

9 seeing his opportunity

10 new weapons

11 as little as sparrows upset eagles

12 truth

13 overloaded with double charges

14 as if they intended to swim in the blood they shed, or re-enact an image of the Crucifixion

15 your words recommend you as much as your wounds; both are honourable

16 he looks like a man in a hurry

Enter ROSS

ROSS   God save the king!

DUNCAN Whence cam'st thou, worthy thane?

ROSS   From Fife, great king;

(1) Where the Norweyan banners flout the sky

And fan our people cold.   **60**

Norway himself, with terrible numbers,

Assisted by that most disloyal traitor

The Thane of Cawdor, began a dismal conflict;

Till that (2) Bellona's bridegroom, (3) lapp'd in proof,

(4) Confronted him with self-comparisons,   **65**

Point against point rebellious, arm 'gainst arm,

Curbing his lavish spirit; and, to conclude,

The victory fell on us.

DUNCAN   Great happiness!

ROSS That now   **70**

Sweno, the Norway's king, (5) craves composition;

Nor would we deign him burial of his men

Till he (6) disbursed, at Saint Colmes-inch,

Ten thousand dollars to our general use.

DUNCAN No more that Thane of Cawdor shall deceive   **75**

Our bosom interest: – go pronounce his present death,

And with his former title greet (7) Macbeth.

ROSS I'll see it done.

DUNCAN What he hath lost, noble Macbeth hath won.   *Exeunt.*

ACT ONE, SCENE THREE

A HEATH

Thunder. Enter the three Witches.

1 WITCH Where hast thou been, sister?

2 WITCH Killing swine.

3 WITCH Sister, where thou?

1 WITCH A Sailor's wife had chestnuts in her lap,

And mounch'd and mounch'd and mounch'd: – *Give me,* quoth I: **5**

(8)*Aroint thee, witch!* the (9) rump-fed ronyon cries.

Her husband's to Aleppo gone, master o' the Tiger:

(10) But in a sieve I'll thither sail,

And, like a rat without a tail,

I'll do, I'll do, and I'll do.   **10**

1   Fife, where the banners
    of the Norwegians seem
    to insult the sky, and our
    people are chilled by the
    wind they create.

2   Goddess of War. Macbeth
    is the bridegroom of the
    Goddess. One of the
    first of many
    acknowledgments of
    his courage.

3   encased in impenetrable
    armour

4   met him face to face with
    equal warlike skills

5   wishes to make terms

6   handed out

7   Ironic, in that Duncan
    gives the traitor's title to
    his saviour Macbeth, so
    soon to betray him.

8   Begone! (a term used in
    exorcism)

9   fat-bottomed hag!

10 Witches were thought to
    be able to sail safely in
    sieves, also to be able to
    transform themselves at
    will into animals, but not
    to be able to achieve tails!

2 WITCH I'll give thee a [1] wind.

1 WITCH Thou art kind.

3 WITCH And I another.

1 WITCH [2] I myself have all the other;

And the very ports they blow,   **15**

All the quarters that they know

I' the shipman's card.

I will drain him dry as hay:

[3] Sleep shall neither night nor day

Hang upon his pent-house lid;   **20**

He shall live a man forbid:

Weary [4] seven-nights nine times nine

Shall he dwindle, peak, and pine:

Though his bark cannot be lost,

Yet it shall be tempest-tost.–   **25**

Look what I have.

2 WITCH Show me, show me.

1 WITCH Here I have a pilot's thumb,

Wreck'd as homeward he did come.

                                  (Drum within.

3 WITCH A drum, a drum!   **30**

[5] Macbeth doth come.

ALL The [6] weird sisters, hand in hand,

[7] Posters of the sea and land,

Thus do go about, about:

Thrice to thine, and thrice to mine,   **35**

And thrice again, to make up nine:–

Peace! – the charm's wound up.

Enter MACBETH *and* BANQUO.

MACBETH So [8] foul and fair a day I have not seen.

BANQUO How far is't call'd to Forres? – What are these,

So wither'd, and so wild in their attire,   **40**

[9] That look not like the inhabitants o' the earth,

And yet are on't? – Live you? or are you aught

That man may question? You seem to under-stand me,

By each at once her [10] chappy finger laying

Upon her skinny lips: – you should be women,   **45**

[11] And yet your beards forbid me to interpret

That you are so.

MACBETH Speak, if you can; – what are you?

1 WITCH All hail, Macbeth! hail to thee, Thane of Glamis!

---

1 Witches could control the winds, and were said to sell them.

2 I own the very ports they blow from, and all the points of the sailor's compass

3 These prophetic lines are echoed later, cf. Act II, sc. ii, 42-51; Act III, sc. ii, 20-26. Pent-house lid - eye-lid.

4 a week

5 The Witches have foreknowledge of Macbeth's approach here, as they did in Act I, sc. i.

6 sisters of Destiny

7 swift travellers

8 Here Macbeth echoes the Witches in Act I, sc. i, 11.

9 Confusion again surrounds the Witches; are they human or inhuman? Male or female? Macbeth is unworried by such details, seeing, or hearing, only what he wishes to see or hear.

10 chapped

11 as 9. The deception practised by the Witches starts here.

2 WITCH All hail, Macbeth! hail to thee,
    Thane of Cawdor!   **50**
3 WITCH All hail, Macbeth! that shalt be king hereafter!
BANQUO Good sir, why do you start; and seem to fear
    (1) Things that do sound so fair? – I' the name of truth,
    Are ye *(2)* fantastical, or that indeed   **55**
    Which outwardly ye show? My noble partner
    You greet with *(3)* present grace and great prediction
    Of noble having and of royal hope,
    That he seems rapt withal: – to me you speak not:
    (4) If you can look into the seeds of time,   **60**
    And say which grain will grow, and which will not,
    Speak then to me, who neither beg nor fear
    Your favours nor your hate.
1 WITCH Hail!
2 WITCH Hail!   **65**
3 WITCH Hail!
1 WITCH Lesser than Macbeth, and greater.
2 WITCH Not so happy, yet much happier.
3 WITCH Thou shalt *(5)* get kings, though thou be none:
    So, all hail, Macbeth and Banquo!   **70**
1 WITCH Banquo and Macbeth, all hail!
MACBETH Stay, you imperfect speakers, tell me more:
    By Sinel's death I know I am Thane of Glamis;
    But how of Cawdor? the Thane of Cawdor lives,
    A prosperous gentleman; and *(6)* to be king   **75**
    Stands not within the prospect of belief,
    No more than to be Cawdor. Say from whence
    You owe this strange intelligence? or why
    Upon this blasted heath you stop our way
    With such prophetic greeting? – Speak, I charge you.   **80**
                        (Witches *vanish.*
BANQUO The earth hath bubbles, as the water has,
    And these are of them: – whither are they vanish'd?
MACBETH Into the air; and what seem'd corporal melted
    As breath into the wind. – Would they had stay'd!
BANQUO Were such things here as we do speak about?   **85**
    Or have we eaten on the *(7)* insane root
    That takes the reason prisoner?
MACBETH *(8)* Your children shall be kings.
BANQUO   *(9)* You shall be king.
MACBETH And Thane of Cawdor too; went it not so?   **90**

1 Banquo's comment underlines his suspicion of deception, and the gulf between appearance and reality. Macbeth's fear is rather fear at what the prophecies suggest to him than of the creatures themselves.

2 imaginary

3 You greet him as one with nobility now, and with hopes of royalty in the future.

4 Demons had the power to see the future; Banquo's question still leaves in doubt what their nature is, therefore.

5 be the father of

6 To be called King is no more credible a prospect than to be called Cawdor. Macbeth has not yet heard of Cawdor's disgrace, so that his surprise when hailed by Ross under that title gives him added motive for hailing the Witches' comments as revelatory and therefore true.

7 a plant, such as hemlock or deadly nightshade, which causes madness

8 The fact that Banquo's children shall rule strikes Macbeth vividly, and becomes an increasing pre-occupation later in the play.

9 Banquo ignores the comment on himself, and reverts to Macbeth's kingship.

BANQUO To the self-same tune and words. Who's here?

Enter ROSS *and* ANGUS

ROSS The king hath happily receiv'd, Macbeth,
The news of thy success: and when he reads
Thy personal venture in the rebels' fight,
(1) His wonders and his praises do contend   **95**
Which should be thine or his: silenc'd with that,
In viewing o'er the rest o' the self-same day,
He finds thee in the stout Norweyan ranks.
(2) Nothing afeard of what thyself didst make,
Strange images of death. As thick as hail   **100**
Came (3) post with post; and every one did bear
Thy praises in his kingdom's great defence,
And pour'd them down before him.

ANGUS   We are sent
To give thee, from our royal master, thanks;   **105**
Only to herald thee into his sight,
Not pay thee.

ROSS And, for an (4) earnest of a greater honour,
He bade me, from him, call thee Thane of Cawdor:
In which addition, hail, most worthy thane!   **110**
For it is thine.

BANQUO   What, can the (5) devil speak true?

MACBETH The Thane of Cawdor lives: why do you (6) dress me
In borrow'd robes?

ANGUS   Who was the thane lives yet;   **115**
But under heavy judgment bears that life
Which he deserves to lose. Whether he was combin'd
With those of Norway, or did line the rebel
With hidden help and vantage, or that with both
He labour'd in his country's wreck, I know not;   **120**
But treasons capital, confess'd and prov'd,
Have overthrown him.

MACBETH   Glamis, and Thane of Cawdor:
(7) The greatest is behind *(aside).* – Thanks for your pains. –
Do you not hope your children shall be kings,   **125**
When those that gave the Thane of Cawdor to me
Promis'd no less to them?

BANQUO   That, (8) trusted home,
Might yet enkindle you unto the crown,
Besides the Thane of Cawdor. But 'tis strange: **130**

1 He cannot decide
   whether to wonder at
   your achievements, or
   load you with his praise.

2 One of many images of
   Macbeth's courage, but in
   itself also ironic in view
   of the later 'images of
   death' that Macbeth
   creates, and his fear of
   them then.

3 message after message

4 a token

5 Banquo clearly sees the
   Witches as diabolical
   now; Macbeth, although
   his shock is as profound,
   reacts more naively with
   curiosity about the
   reason for the title.

6 The first of many images
   of clothing, which are
   part of the theme of
   deception and false
   appearances.

7 the greatest prophecy is
   yet to be fulfilled

8 taken to heart

And [1] oftentimes to win us to our harm,
  The instruments of darkness tell us truths;
  Win us with honest trifles, to betray's
  In deepest consequence. –
  [2] Cousins, a word, I pray you.   135

MACBETH   Two truths are told,
  As happy prologues to the swelling act
  [3] Of the imperial theme *(aside.)* – I thank you, gentlemen. –
  This [4] supernatural soliciting   *(Aside.*
  [5] Cannot be ill; cannot be good: – if ill,   140
  Why hath it given me earnest of success,
  Commencing in a truth? I am Thane of Cawdor:
  If good, why do I yield to that suggestion
  Whose [6] horrid image doth unfix my hair,
  And make my [7] seated heart knock at my ribs,   145
  Against the use of nature? Present fears
  Are less than horrible imaginings:
  My thought, whose murder yet is but [8] fantastical,
  Shakes so my [9] single state of man, that [10] function
  Is smother'd in surmise; and nothing is   150
  But what is not.

BANQUO   Look, how our partner's rapt.

MACBETH *(Aside.)* [11] If chance will have me king,
  Why, chance may crown me,
  Without my stir.   155

BANQUO   New honours come upon him,
  [12] Like our strange garments, cleave not to their mould
  But with the aid of use.

MACBETH *(Aside.)*   Come what come may,
  Time and the hour runs through the roughest day.   160

BANQUO Worthy Macbeth, we stay upon your leisure.

MACBETH Give me your favour: – my dull brain was wrought
  With things forgotten. Kind gentlemen, your pains
  Are register'd where every day I turn
  The leaf to read them. – Let us toward the king. –   165
  Think upon what hath chanc'd; and, at more time,
  The [13] interim having weigh'd it, let us speak
  Our free hearts each to other.

BANQUO   Very gladly.

MACBETH Till then, enough. – Come, friends.   *Exeunt.*   170

---

1 often the powers of evil convince us with trivial truths, in order to deceive us later in profound matters

2 'cousins' does not imply relationship here, but friendship

3 These words reveal that Macbeth has travelled a long way towards seeing his own power as king as a definite aim, and one whose achievement is actually underway. His air of certainty is striking.

4 suggestion by the powers of evil

5 He has certainly not understood Banquo's warning, and seems to be capable of admitting that the prophecies are evil in origin, yet may not be evil in their nature!

6 of death and murder

7 fixed heart beat in an unnatural way

8 in the imagination

9 my sense of moral integrity

10 the power to act is stifled by contradictory notions

11 He is deceiving himself here, as in his next speech, by seeming to reject involvement in the process of gaining the crown.

12 another image of unfamiliar clothing which appears not to fit

13 having had time to consider it at leisure

ACT ONE, SCENE FOUR
FORRES – A ROOM IN THE PALACE

Flourish. Enter DUNCAN, MALCOLM, DONALBAIN, LENNOX *and*
Attendants.

DUNCAN Is execution done on Cawdor? Are not	
Those in commission yet return'd?	
MALCOLM My liege,	
They are not yet come back. But I have spoke	
With one that saw him die: who did report,	5
That very frankly he confess'd his treasons;	
Implor'd your highness' pardon; and *(1)* set forth	
A deep repentance: nothing in his life	
Became him like the leaving it; he died	
As one that had been studied in his death,	10
(2) To throw away the dearest thing he ow'd,	
As 'twere a careless trifle.	
DUNCAN There's *(3)* no art	
To find the mind's construction in the face:	
He was a gentleman on whom I built	15
An absolute trust. –	

Enter MACBETH, BANQUO, ROSS *and* ANGUS.

O worthiest cousin!
The sin of my ingratitude even now
Was heavy on me: thou art *(4)* so far before,
That swiftest wing of recompense is slow   20
To overtake thee. *(5)* Would thou hadst less deserv'd;
That the proportion both of thanks and payment
Might have been mine! only I have left to say,
More is thy due than more than all can pay.
MACBETH The service and the loyalty I owe,   25
In doing it, pays itself. Your highness' part
Is to receive our duties: and *(6)* our duties
Are to your throne and state children and servants;
Which do but what they should, by doing everything
Safe toward your love and honour.   30
DUNCAN Welcome hither:
I have begun to plant thee, and will labour
To make thee full of growing. – Noble Banquo,
That hast no less deserv'd, nor must be known

1 professed

2 carelessly casting his life away as if it meant nothing to him

3 No skills can interpret the face so as to read the mind. Duncan's trust in Macbeth is deeply ironic, particularly in view of Lady Macbeth's later advice to her husband to 'look like the innocent flower but be the serpent under't.

4 Your merits are so great that my rewards cannot catch up with them.

5 If only you had deserved less, I might have been able to reward you as I think fits·your achievement.

6 Macbeth can only mouth conventionalities here. His protestations of loyalty and service seem ironically insincere to the audience, even before Lady Macbeth has turned his imagination into reality.

(1) No less to have done so, let me infold thee,   35
And hold thee to my heart.
BANQUO   There if I grow,
The harvest is your own.
DUNCAN   My *(2)* plenteous joys,
Wanton in fulness, seek to hide themselves   40
In drops of sorrow. – Sons, kinsmen, thanes,
And you whose places are the nearest, know,
We will *(3)* establish our estate upon
Our eldest, Malcolm; whom we name here-after
The Prince of Cumberland: which *(4)* honour must   45
Not unaccompanied invest him only,
But signs of nobleness, like stars, shall shine
On all deservers. – From hence to Inverness,
And bind us further to you.
MACBETH The *(5)* rest is labour, which is not us'd for you: 50
I'll be myself the *(6)* harbinger, and make joyful
The hearing of my wife with your approach;
So, humbly take my leave.
DUNCAN My worthy Cawdor!
MACBETH *(Aside.)* The Prince of Cumberland! – That is a step,   55
On which I must fall down, or else o'er-leap,
For in my way it lies. Stars, hide your fires!
Let not light see my black and deep desires:
(7) The eye wink at the hand! yet let that be,
Which the eye fears, when it is done, to see.   *(Exit.*   60
DUNCAN True, worthy Banquo, – he is full so valiant;
(8) And in his commendations I am fed, –
It is a banquet to me. Let us after him,
Whose care is gone before to bid us welcome:
It is a peerless kinsman.   *(Flourish. Exeunt.*   65

1	and must equally be publicly applauded for your deeds
2	my joy is so great and overflowing that it makes me weep
3	settle the succession
4	His must not be the only merit to be rewarded. The beneficent formality of Duncan's kingship may be coveted by Macbeth, but never attained, ironically.
5	to serve you is to be at rest
6	messenger sent ahead to make arrangements
7	Let the eye not see what the hand does. The first of many invocations of darkness and acknowledgements that Macbeth would prefer not to recognise his own actions.
8	Duncan's delight in praising Macbeth rings ironically after Macbeth's last aside.

ACT ONE, SCENE FIVE
INVERNESS – A ROOM IN MACBETH'S CASTLE

Enter LADY MACBETH, *reading a letter.*

LADY MACBETH *They met me in the day of success; and I have learned by the perfectest report, they have more in them than mortal knowledge. When I burned in desire to question them further, they made themselves air, into which they vanished. Whiles I*

stood rapt in the wonder of it, came missives from the king, who 5
all-hailed me, Thane of Cawdor; by which title, before, these
weird sisters saluted me, and referred me to the [1] *coming on of*
time, with Hail, king that shalt be! *This have I thought good to*
deliver thee, my dearest partner of greatness, that thou mightst
not lose the [2] *dues of rejoicing, by being ignorant of what* 10
greatness is promised thee. Lay it to thy heart, and farewell.

Glamis thou art, and Cawdor; and shalt be
What thou art promis'd: yet do I fear thy nature;
It is [3] too full o' the milk of human kindness
To catch the nearest way: thou wouldst be great; 15
Art not without ambition; but without
The [4] illness should attend it. What thou wouldst highly,
That wouldst thou holily; wouldst not play false,
And yet wouldst wrongly win: thou'dst [5] have, great Glamis,
That which cries, *Thus thou must do, if thou have it:* 20
And that which rather thou dost fear to do
Than wishest should be undone. Hie thee hither,
That I may pour my spirits in thine ear;
And chastise with the valour of my tongue
All that impedes thee from the [6] golden round, 25
Which fate and [7] metaphysical aid doth seem
To have thee crown'd withal.

Enter an Attendant.
                                        What is your tidings?
ATTENDANT The king comes here to-night.
LADY MACBETH   Thou'rt mad to say it: 30
Is not thy master with him? who, were't so,
[8] Would have inform'd for preparation.
ATTENDANT So please you, it is true: – our thane is coming:
One of my fellows had the speed of him;
Who, almost dead for breath, had scarcely more 35
Than would make up his message.
LADY MACBETH   Give him tending,
He brings great news.   *Exit Attendant.*
[9] The raven himself is hoarse
That croaks the fatal entrance of Duncan 40
Under my battlements. Come, you spirits
That tend on [10] mortal thoughts, unsex me here;
And fill me, from the crown to the toe, top-full
Of direst cruelty! make thick my blood,

1 the future

2 the rejoicing due to you

3 your nature is too aware
   of humane feelings to
   seize the obvious
   opportunity (compare
   Act IV, sc.iii, 110; I, v, 49)

4 you lack the ruthlessness
   that needs to go with
   ambition

5 you long to possess the
   crown, without doing the
   deed to gain it; you fear
   to do that deed, but you
   still wish it done

6 the crown

7 supernatural aid

8 would have informed me
   so that I could have
   prepared

9 An appalling list of
   images of evil,
   culminating in a vision of
   herself with the murder
   weapon. It is as if Lady
   Macbeth needs the
   stimulus of these
   horrors, which her
   husband cannot bear to
   envisage.

10 ideas, intentions, of
    murder or death

(1) Stop up the access and passage to remorse,   45

That no compunctious visitings of nature

Shake my fell purpose, nor keep peace between

The effect and it! Come to my woman's breasts,

And take my milk for gall, you *(2)* murdering ministers,

Wherever in your *(3)* sightless substances   50

You wait on nature's mischief! Come, thick night,

And *(4)* pall thee in the dunnest smoke of hell,

That my keen knife see not the wound it makes,

Nor heaven peep through the blanket of the dark,

To cry, *Hold, hold!*   55

Enter MACBETH

Great Glamis! worthy Cawdor!

Greater than both, by the all-hail hereafter!

Thy letters have transported me beyond

This ignorant present, and I feel now

The future in the instant.   60

MACBETH   My dearest love,

Duncan comes here to-night.

LADY MACBETH   And when goes hence?

MACBETH To-morrow, – as he purposes.

LADY MACBETH   O, never   65

Shall sun that morrow see!

(5) Your face, my thane, is as a book where men

May read strange matters: – to *(6)* beguile the time,

Look like the time; bear welcome in your eye,

Your hand, your tongue: look like the innocent flower,   70

But be the serpent under't. He that's coming

Must be provided for: and you shall put

This night's great business into my *(7)* despatch;

Which shall to all our nights and days to come

Give solely sovereign sway and masterdom.   75

MACBETH We will speak further.

LADY MACBETH   Only look up clear;

To alter favour ever is to fear:

Leave all the rest to me.   *Exeunt.*

---

1 Thicken my blood so that pity cannot enter - then no feeling of human compassion will shake my sense of purpose, or come between it and its longed-for outcome. Her reference to milk, natural nourishment between mother and child, recalls her comment on Macbeth in her first speech.

2 evil spirits which motivate murder

3 invisible forms

4 wrap yourselves (as in a funeral shroud)

These lines reveal Lady Macbeth's sense of sin, conscience and retribution, but she invokes the powers of evil and darkness to conceal and stifle them. Compare Macbeth's response to the dagger and his fear of divine retribution.

5 These lines recall Duncan's comment 'There's no art/To find the mind's construction in the face', and look forward to Lady Macbeth's 'Look like the innocent flower/But be the serpent under't'.

6 in order to control the present, adopt an appearance suitable to it

7 control, organisation: ironic lines because of the double meanings of 'provided for', 'business' and 'despatch'

ACT ONE, SCENE SIX
THE SAME – BEFORE THE CASTLE

Hautboys and torches. Servants of MACBETH *attending.*
Enter DUNCAN, MALCOLM, DONALBAIN, BANQUO, LENNOX, MACDUFF,
ROSS, ANGUS *and* Attendants.

DUNCAN This castle hath a pleasant seat: the air
  Nimbly and sweetly recommends itself
  Unto our gentle senses.
BANQUO This guest of summer,
  The temple-haunting *(1)* martlet, does approve,   5
  By his lov'd mansionry, that *(2)* the heaven's breath
  Smells wooingly here: no *(3)* jutty, frieze, buttress,
  Nor coigne of vantage, but this bird hath made
  His *(4)* pendant bed and procreant cradle:
  Where they most breed and haunt, I have observ'd   10
  The air is delicate.

  Enter LADY MACBETH.
DUNCAN   See, see, our honour'd hostess! –
  (5) The love that follows us sometime is our trouble,
  Which still we thank as love. Herein I teach you
  How you shall bid God 'ild us for your pains,   15
  And thank us for your trouble.
LADY MACBETH   All our service
  In every point twice done, and then done double,
  Were poor and single business to contend
  Against those honours deep and broad where-with   20
  Your majesty loads our house: for those of old,
  And the late dignities heap'd up to them,
  (6) We rest your hermits.
DUNCAN   Where's the Thane of Cawdor?
  We *(7)* cours'd him at the heels, and had a purpose   25
  To be his purveyor: but he rides well;
  (8) And his great love, sharp as his spur, hath holp him
  To his home before us. Fair and noble hostess,
  We are your guest to-night.
LADY MACBETH   Your servants ever   30
  (9) Have theirs, themselves, and what is theirs, in compt,
  To make their audit at your highness' pleasure,
  Still to return your own.

1 house martin
2 The irony of this scene is ubiquitous; Duncan and Banquo cannot express too forcefully their impressions of the welcoming and even blessed air of Macbeth's castle, while the audience remains strongly aware of the sinister intentions of their host and hostess. This is true dramatic irony, when the writer juxtaposes the audience's understanding with that of the innocence or misunderstanding of a character or characters on the stage.
3 'jutty . . . coigne' - architectural terms for features of the castle
4 hanging nest, a cradle for its young
5 My followers' love for me sometimes causes me trouble, but I am still grateful for that love. So you must be taught by my example to ask God to bless me for the trouble that I cause you.
6 for past honours, and those recently added to them, we are your grateful servants and pray for you - Lady Macbeth's uneasy hyperboles here can be compared with Macbeth's in Act I, sc. iv, 25-30
7 pursued at his heels
8 Further irony in Duncan's conviction of Macbeth's love for him.
9 We, your servants, keep all that we have in readiness so that you can at any time call on us for what is, by rights, your own.

DUNCAN   Give me your hand;
Conduct me to mine host: we love him highly,   35
And shall continue our graces towards him.
By your leave, hostess.   *Exeunt.*

ACT ONE, SCENE SEVEN

THE SAME — A LOBBY IN THE CASTLE

Hautboys and torches. Enter, and pass over, a Sewer, *and divers*
Servants *with dishes and service. Then enter* MACBETH.

MACBETH If it were done when 'tis done, then 'twere well
It were done quickly. [1] If the assassination
Could trammel up the consequence, and catch,
With his surcease, success; that but this blow
Might be the be-all and the end-all here,   5
But here, upon this bank and shoal of time, –
We'd jump the life to come. But in these cases
We still have judgment here; that we but teach
Bloody instructions, which being taught, return
To plague the inventor: this even-handed justice   10
Commands the ingredients of our poison'd chalice
To our own lips. He's here in double trust:
First, as I am his kinsman and his subject,
Strong both against the deed: then, as his host,
Who should against his murderer shut the door,   15
Not bear the knife myself. Besides, this Duncan
Hath [2] borne his faculties so meek, hath been
So clear in his great office, that his virtues
Will plead like angels, trumpet-tongued, against
The [3] deep damnation of his taking-off: 20
And pity, like a naked new-born babe,
Striding the blast, or heaven's cherubin, [4] hors'd
Upon the sightless couriers of the air,
Shall blow the horrid deed in every eye,
That tears shall drown the wind. – I have no spur   25
To prick the sides of my intent, but only
[5] Vaulting ambition, which o'er leaps itself,
And falls on the other.

1 If the deed was over when the murder was completed, then it would be best to do it quickly. If the killing could end the matter, preventing consequences, so that his death was final, the death blow finalising the action, here, just here, upon this little island in eternity, I'd risk what was to come. But in such cases we receive sentence here, in that we set in motion further bloodshed for which, as initiator, we must accept retribution; impartial justice makes us drink the poisoned cup that we have prepared for others.

2 he has carried out his kingly responsibilities so modestly
Macbeth here marshals, with a control and logic we do not see again in him, the compelling reasons why he should not kill the king. Only ambition, as he says, and Lady Macbeth, as we know, can combine to overturn the argument, so strong is it.

3 the damnable deed of his murder

4 astride the wind - his revulsion at the thought of murder, and recognition of the pity it would evoke, express themselves in apocryphal imagery

5 He has no grievances to spur him on, indeed, only bonds with Duncan. His recognition that ambition may over-reach itself and so fall, is prophetic, and so, ironic.

Enter LADY MACBETH

                     How now! what news?

LADY MACBETH He has almost supp'd: why have you left the chamber?   30

MACBETH Hath he ask'd for me?

LADY MACBETH   Know you not he has?

MACBETH We will proceed no further in this business:
       He hath honour'd me of late; and I have bought
       Golden opinions from all sorts of people,   35
       Which would be worn now in their newest gloss,
       Not cast aside so soon.

LADY MACBETH   Was the hope drunk
       Wherein you dress'd yourself? hath it slept since?
       And wakes it now, to look so green and pale   40
       At what it did so freely? From this time
       Such I account thy love. Art thou afeard
       To be the same in thine own act and valour
       As thou art in desire? Wouldst thou have that
       Which thou esteem'st the [1] ornament of life,   45
       And live a coward in thine own esteem;
       Letting [2] *I dare not* wait upon *I would,*
       Like the poor cat i' the adage?

MACBETH   Pr'ythee, peace:
       [3] I dare do all that may become a man;   50
       Who dares do more is none.

LADY MACBETH   What beast was't, then,
       That made you break this enterprise to me?
       When you durst do it, then you were a man;
       And, to be more than what you were, you would   55
       Be so much more the man. Nor time nor place
       Did then adhere, and yet you would make both:
       They have made themselves, and that their fitness now
       Does unmake you. [4] I have given suck, and know
       How tender 'tis to love the babe that milks me: 60
       I would, while it was smiling in my face,
       Have pluck'd my nipple from his boneless gums,
       And dash'd the brains out, had I so sworn as you
       Have done to this.

MACBETH   If we should fail?   65

LADY MACBETH   We fail!
       But screw your courage to the [5] sticking place,
       And we'll not fail. When Duncan is asleep, –
       Whereto the rather shall this day's hard journey

---

1   the crown. But this is again ironic, since by striving for the crown, Macbeth loses the peace of a calm conscience, which should be 'the ornament of life'.

2   letting your fear dominate your ambition like the cat in the proverb. (The cat wanted to catch fish but was afraid to get its feet wet!)

3   Macbeth's moral perception that the murder is not manly but *bestial*, is horrifyingly countered by his wife's argument that the action would be *heroically* manly ('so much more the man'). Similarly, her use of the imagery of 'making' and 'unmaking' is profoundly disturbing in its effectiveness. In fact, as soon as he embarks on the course of action she advocates, he is 'unmade'.

4   These lines, revealing that Lady Macbeth has had a child, have caused many critical hypotheses in the past. In this context, however, what is important is that she uses the strength of the natural bond between mother and child, and her own ability to have broken that bond in order to hold to her resolution (in imagination), as a strong argument to persuade her husband to continue in his resolve to murder the king (against his feeling of natural bonds too strong to be infringed). Her chilling comment re-introduces the theme of parents and children which continues throughout the play.

5   the point at which a cross-bow's cord stays in position. A good military metaphor for courage, and likely to appeal to Macbeth.

Soundly invite him, his two chamberlains   70
Will I with wine and *(1)* wassail so convince
(2) That memory, the warder of the brain,
Shall be a fume, and the receipt of reason
A limbec only: when in swinish sleep
Their *(3)* drenched natures lie as in a death,   75
What cannot you and I perform upon
The unguarded Duncan? what not put upon
His spongy officers; who shall bear the guilt
Of our great *(4)* quell?

MACBETH   Bring forth men-children only;   80
For thy undaunted mettle should compose
Nothing but males. Will it not be receiv'd
(5) When we have mark'd with blood those sleepy two
Of his own chamber, and us'd their very daggers,
That they have done't?   85

LADY MACBETH   Who dares receive it other,
As we shall make our griefs and clamour roar
Upon his death?

MACBETH   I am settled, and bend up
Each *(6)* corporal agent to this terrible feat.   90
Away, and mock the time with fairest show:
False face must hide what the false heart doth know.   *Exeunt.*

Notes:

1 carousing, drinking of healths
2 memory will be confused and will prevent the functioning of reason
3 dosed, drowned; poisoned with wine
4 killing
5 Macbeth's delight in the deception shows his new resolve to do evil.
6 bodily faculty

ACT TWO, SCENE ONE

INVERNESS – COURT WITHIN THE CASTLE

Enter BANQUO, *preceded by* FLEANCE *with a torch.*

BANQUO How goes the night, boy?
FLEANCE The moon is down; I have not heard the clock.
BANQUO And she goes down at twelve.
FLEANCE I take't, 'tis later, sir.
BANQUO Hold, take my sword. – There's *(7)* husbandry in heaven;   5
Their candles are all out: – take thee that too. –
A heavy summons lies like lead upon me,
And yet I would not sleep: – merciful powers,
Restrain me in the *(8)* cursed thoughts that nature
Gives way to in repose! – Give me my sword.   10

7 economy. Banquo refers to the unnatural darkness of the night; Lady Macbeth's appeal for blackness has been heard.
8 Banquo too has disturbed sleep. We are reminded of the Witches' ability to prevent sleep and provide 'cursed thoughts', which will be very clearly seen in Macbeth in Act II, sc. ii, 50-51 and Act III, sc. ii, 21-22.

Who's there?

Enter MACBETH, *and a* Servant *with a torch.*

MACBETH A friend.

BANQUO What, sir, not yet at rest? The king's a-bed:
He hath been in unusual pleasure, and
Sent forth great (1) largess to your officers: 15
This diamond he greets your wife withal,
By the name of most kind hostess; and (2) shut up
In measureless content.

MACBETH   Being unprepar'd,
(3) Our will became the servant to defect;   20
Which else should free have wrought.

BANQUO   All's well.
I dreamt last night of the three weird sisters:
To you they have show'd some truth.

MACBETH   I think not of them: 25
Yet, when we can entreat an hour to serve,
We would spend it in some words upon that business,
If you would grant the time.

BANQUO   At your kind'st leisure.

MACBETH If you shall (4) cleave to my consent, – when 'tis,   30
It shall make honour for you.

BANQUO   (5) So I lose none
In seeking to augment it, but still keep
My bosom franchis'd, and allegiance clear,
I shall be counsell'd.   35

MACBETH   Good repose the while!

BANQUO Thanks, sir; the like to you!   *Exeunt* BANQUO *and* FLEANCE.

MACBETH Go bid thy mistress, when my drink is ready,
She strike upon the bell. Get thee to bed.   *Exit* Servant.
Is this a dagger which I see before me,   40
The handle toward my hand? Come, let me clutch thee:-
I have thee not, and yet I see thee still.
(6) Art thou not, fatal vision, sensible
To feeling as to sight? or art thou but
A dagger of the mind, a false creation,   45
Proceeding from the heart-oppressed brain?
I see thee yet, in form as palpable
As this which now I draw.
Thou marshall'st me the way that I was going;
And such an instrument I was to use.   50

1 generous gifts

2 concluded his evening

3 our service was not as
    efficient as we would
    have wished

4 support me

5 As long as I lose no
    honour by attempting to
    increase it, but can
    continue to do my duty
    guiltlessly (to the King), I
    shall take your advice.

6 This vision of a dagger,
    another example of
    unreal seeming, proceeds
    from Macbeth's own
    imagination, heightened
    as it is by guilt and
    horror

(1) Mine eyes are made the fools o' the other senses.
Or else worth all the rest: <u>I see thee still;</u>
<u>And on thy blade and (2) dudgeon gouts of blood,</u>
<u>Which was not so before.</u> – There's no such thing:
<u>It is the bloody business which informs</u>   55
<u>Thus to mine eyes.</u> – Now o'er the one-half world
Nature seems dead, and wicked dreams abuse
The curtain'd sleep; now witchcraft celebrates
Pale (3) Hecate's offerings; and wither'd murder,
<u>Alarum'd by his sentinel, the wolf,</u>   60
<u>Whose howl's his watch, thus with his stealthy pace,</u>
With (4) Tarquin's ravishing strides, towards his design
<u>Moves like a ghost.</u> – Thou sure and firm-set earth,
Hear not my steps, which way they walk, <u>for fear</u>
<u>The very stones prate of my whereabout,</u>   65
And (5) take the present horror from the time,
Which now suits with it. – Whiles I threat, he lives;
Words to the heat of deeds too cold breath gives.   *(A bell rings.*
I go, and it is done; the bell invites me.
Hear it not, Duncan, for it is a knell   70
That summons thee to heaven or to hell.   *Exit.*

1 Either my eyes are at
fault, my other senses
being reliable, or they are
worth all the rest

2 hilt

3 Hecate is Goddess of the
night, ghosts and witches

4 Tarquin, in Roman
legend, was the
nobleman who raped
Lucretia, as in
Shakespeare's 'Rape of
Lucrece'.

5 Macbeth is afraid that the
stones on which he walks
will retain the sound of
his guilty steps, and be
able to recreate the
horror of the moment on
future occasions.

ACT TWO, SCENE TWO

INVERNESS – COURT WITHIN THE CASTLE

Enter LADY MACBETH

LADY MACBETH That which hath made them drunk hath made me bold:
What hath quench'd them hath given me fire. – Hark! – Peace!
<u>It was the owl that shriek'd, the fatal bellman,</u>
Which gives the stern'st good-night. He is about it:
The doors are open; and the surfeited grooms   5
Do (6) mock their charge with snores: I have drugg'd their (7) possets,
That death and nature do contend about them,
Whether they live or die.
MACBETH *(Within.)*   Who's there? – what, ho!
LADY MACBETH Alack! I am afraid they have awak'd,   10
And 'tis not done: – the attempt, and not the deed,
Confounds us. – Hark! – I laid their daggers ready;
He could not miss 'em. – (8) <u>Had he not resembled</u>

6 make a mockery of their
duty (to guard the King)
by sleeping drunkenly

7 hot drinks

8 This sudden revelation of
Lady Macbeth's stifled
tenderness shocks us, but
also prepares for her
break-down in the sleep-
walking scene.

My father as he slept, I had done't. – My husband!

Re-enter MACBETH

MACBETH [1] I have done the deed. – Didst thou not hear a noise?   15

LADY MACBETH I heard the owl scream and the crickets cry.
Did not you speak?

MACBETH   When?

LADY MACBETH   Now.

MACBETH   As I descended?   20

LADY MACBETH Ay.

MACBETH Hark! –
Who lies i' the second chamber?

LADY MACBETH   Donalbain.

MACBETH This is a sorry sight.   *(Looking on his hands.*   25

LADY MACBETH A foolish thought to say a sorry sight.

MACBETH There's one did laugh in's sleep, and one cried *Murder!*
That they did wake each other: I stood and heard them:
But they did say their prayers, and [2] address'd them
Again to sleep.   30

LADY MACBETH There are two lodg'd together.

MACBETH One cried, *God bless us!* and, *Amen,* the other;
As they had seen me with these hangman's hands.
Listening their fear, I could not say, *Amen,*
When they did say, *God bless us.*   35

LADY MACBETH Consider it not so deeply.

MACBETH But wherefore could I not pronounce *Amen?*
I had most need of blessing, and *Amen*
Stuck in my throat.

LADY MACBETH   These deeds must not be thought   40
After these ways; so, it will make us mad.

MACBETH Methought I heard a voice cry, *Sleep no more!*
Macbeth does murder sleep, – the innocent sleep:
Sleep that [3] knits up the [4] ravell'd sleave of care,
The death of each day's life, sore labour's bath,   45
Balm of hurt minds, [5] great nature's second course,
Chief nourisher in life's feast.

LADY MACBETH   What do you mean?

MACBETH Still it cried, *Sleep no more!* to all the house:
Glamis hath murder'd sleep: and therefore Cawdor   50
Shall sleep no more, – Macbeth shall sleep no more!

LADY MACBETH Who was it that thus cried? Why, worthy thane,
You do unbend your noble strength to think

---

1 Again, Macbeth cannot pronounce the word 'murder', or even 'death', as in Act I, sc. vii.

2 prepared themselves for sleep. Is it the grooms, or the royal brothers, who are referred to?

3 straightens out, unravels
4 tangled silk threads
5 that which follows hard work, as a second course of a meal follows a first

So brainsickly of things. – Go get some water,
And wash this *(1)* filthy witness from your hand. –   55
Why did you bring these daggers from the place?
They must lie there: go carry them; and smear
The sleepy grooms with blood.

MACBETH   I'll go no more:
I am afraid to think what I have done;   60
Look on't again I dare not.

LADY MACBETH   *(2)* Infirm of purpose!
Give me the daggers: *(3)* the sleeping and the dead
Are but as pictures: 'tis the eye of childhood
That fears a painted devil. If he do bleed,   65
I'll gild the faces of the grooms withal,
For it must seem their *(4)* guilt.

                          Exit. (Knocking within.

MACBETH   Whence is that knocking?
How is't with me, when every noise appals me?
What hands are here? Ha! they pluck out mine eyes!   70
Will all great Neptune's ocean wash this blood
Clean from my hand? No: this my hand will rather
The multitudinous seas *(5)* incarnadine,
Making the green one red.

Re-enter LADY MACBETH

LADY MACBETH My hands are of your colour; but I shame   75
To wear a heart so white.   *(Knocking within.*
                    I hear a knocking
At the south entry: – retire we to our chamber.
A little water clears us of this deed:
(6) How easy is it then! Your constancy   80
Hath left you unattended. – Hark! more knocking:
                              (Knocking within.
Get on your nightgown, lest occasion call us,
And show us to be watchers: – be not lost
So poorly in your thoughts.

MACBETH *(7)* To know my deed, 'twere best not know myself.   85
                              (Knocking within.
Wake Duncan with thy knocking! I would thou couldst!
                          Exeunt.

---

1   bloody evidence

2   weak-willed

3   Lady Macbeth's crisp
      admonition is chiefly to
      convince herself, and is a
      piece of self-deception. It
      has no effect as an appeal
      to Macbeth.

4   gild/guilt - a particularly
      chilling pun

5   to make crimson
      (literally, to make flesh-
      coloured)

6   For the full force of this
      ironic optimism, we have
      to see Lady Macbeth's
      frantic efforts to remove
      the blood from her hands
      in the sleep-walking
      scene.

7   It would be better not to
      recognise myself, than to
      acknowledge what I have
      done.

ACT TWO, SCENE THREE
INVERNESS – COURT WITHIN THE CASTLE

Enter a Porter. *(Knocking within.)*

PORTER Here's a knocking indeed! If a man were porter of hell-gate, he
should have (1) old turning the key. *(Knocking.)* Knock, knock,
knock. Who's there, i' the name of (2) Beelzebub? Here's a farmer
that hanged himself on the expectation of plenty: come in time;
have napkins enow about you; here you'll sweat for't. –   5
(Knocking.) Knock, knock! Who's there i' the (3) other devil's name?
Faith, here's an (4) equivocator, that could swear in both the scales
against either scale; who committed treason enough for God's
sake, (5) yet could not equivocate to heaven: O, come in, equivocator.
(Knocking.) Knock, knock, knock! Who's there! Faith, here's an   10
English tailor come hither, for stealing out of a French hose:
come in, tailor, here you may roast your (6) goose. – *(Knocking.)*
Knock, knock: never at quiet! What are you? – But this place is
too cold for hell. I'll devil-porter it no further: I had thought to
have let in some of all professions, that go the primrose way to   15
the everlasting bonfire. *(Knocking.)* Anon, anon! I pray you,
remember the porter.   *(Opens the gate.*

Enter MACDUFF *and* LENNOX.

MACDUFF Was it so late, friend, ere you went to bed, that you
do lie so late?

PORTER Faith, sir, we were carousing till the second cock: 20
and drink, sir, is a great provoker of three things.

MACDUFF What three things does drink especially provoke?

PORTER Marry, sir, (7) nose-painting, sleep, and urine. Lechery, sir, it
provokes and it unprovokes; it (8) provokes the desire, but it takes
away the performance: therefore, (9) much drink may be said to be   25
an equivocator with lechery: it makes him, and it mars him; it
sets him on, and it takes him off; it persuades him, and
disheartens him; makes him stand to, and not stand to: in
conclusion, equivocates him in a sleep, and, (10) giving him the lie,
leaves him.   30

MACDUFF I believe drink gave thee the lie last night.

PORTER That it did, sir, i' the very throat o' me: but I requited him
for his lie; and, I think, being too strong for him, though he took
up my legs sometime, yet (11) I made a shift to cast him.

MACDUFF Is thy master stirring? –   35
Our knocking has awak'd him; here he comes.

1 plenty of key-turning
2 Beelzebub is one of the chief devils
3 Satan
4 a deceiver, particularly one who uses religious terms to deceive
5 an ironic parallel with Macbeth
6 a tailor's iron, which would be heated (roast) on the fire
7 reference to the red or 'strawberry' nose produced by drinking; cf. Bardolph in "Henry V".
8 drink stimulates sexual desire but causes ineptness in its fulfilment. The underlying theme is the distance between imagination and real action, as Macbeth had experienced over the prospect of murdering Duncan.
9 The effect of drink on lust works like a series of delusions, rousing to let fall, exciting only to disappoint.
10 'to give someone the lie' can mean either to throw him flat, as in wrestling, or to deceive
11 managed to throw, or managed to get rid of (drink) by vomiting. The Porter carries on Macduff's development of his own original image.

Enter MACBETH

LENNOX Good-morrow, noble sir!

MACBETH Good-morrow, both!

MACDUFF Is the king stirring, worthy Thane?

MACBETH Not yet.　　　　40

MACDUFF He did command me to call timely on him.
I have almost slipp'd the hour.

MACBETH I'll bring you to him.

MACDUFF I know this is a joyful trouble to you;
But yet 'tis one.　　　　45

MACBETH The labour we delight in *(1)* physics pain.　　　　　　　　*1*　cures
This is the door.

MACDUFF I'll make so bold to call.
For 'tis my limited service.　　*Exit* MACDUFF.

LENNOX Goes the king hence to-day?　　　　50

MACBETH He does: he did appoint so.

LENNOX The night has been unruly: where we lay,
Our chimneys were blown down: and, as they say,
Lamentings heard i' the air; strange screams of death;　　　　*2*　confusion
And prophesying, with accents terrible,　　　　55　　*3*　consequences
Of dire *(2)* combustion and confus'd *(3)* events,　　　　*4*　owl, the bird of darkness
New hatch'd to the woeful time: the *(4)* obscure bird　　　　　　　(obscurity)
Clamour'd the live-long night: some say the earth
Was feverous, and did shake.

MACBETH 'Twas a rough night.　　　　60

LENNOX My young remembrance cannot parallel
A fellow to it.

Re-enter MACDUFF.

MACDUFF O horror, horror, horror! Tongue nor heart
Cannot conceive nor name thee!

MACBETH, LENNOX What's the matter?　　　　65　　*5*　The King. A glance at

MACDUFF Confusion now hath made his masterpiece　　　　　　James Ist's advocacy of
Most sacrilegious murder hath broke ope　　　　　　the Divine Right of
The *(5)* Lord's anointed temple, and stole thence　　　　　　Kings. Shakespeare
The life o' the building.　　　　　　continually stresses the

MACBETH What is't you say? the life?　　　　70　　horror of regicide.

LENNOX Mean you his majesty?　　　　*6*　Classical myth refers to

MACDUFF Approach the chamber, and destroy your sight　　　　three Gorgons, one of
With a new *(6)* Gorgon: – do not bid me speak;　　　　whom, Medusa, was so
See, and then speak yourselves.　　*Exeunt* MACBETH *and* LENNOX.　　visually horrible as to
Awake! awake! –　　　　75　　turn viewers to stone.

Ring the alarum-bell: – murder and treason!
Banquo and Donalbain! Malcolm! awake!
Shake off this downy sleep, death's counterfeit,
And look on death itself! up, up, and see
The [1] great doom's image! Malcolm! Banquo!   **80**
As from your graves rise up, and walk like sprites,
To countenance this horror!

           (Alarum-bell rings.

Re-enter LADY MACBETH

LADY MACBETH   What's the business,
That such a hideous trumpet calls to parley
The sleepers of the house? speak, speak!   **85**

MACDUFF O gentle lady,
 'Tis not for you to hear what I can speak:
 [2] This repetition, in a woman's ear,
 Would murder as it fell.

Re-enter BANQUO

       O Banquo, Banquo!   **90**
Our royal master's murder'd!

LADY MACBETH   Woe, alas!
What, in our house?

BANQUO   Too cruel anywhere. –
Dear Duff, pr'ythee, contradict thyself,   **95**
And say it is not so.

Re-enter MACBETH *and* LENNOX

MACBETH Had I but died an hour before this chance,
I had liv'd a blessed time; for, from this instant,
There's nothing serious in [3] mortality:
All is but [4] toys: renown and grace is dead;   **100**
The wine of life is drawn, and the mere [5] lees
Is left this [6] vault to brag of.

Enter MALCOLM *and* DONALBAIN

DONALBAIN What is amiss?

MACBETH   You are, and do not know't:
 The spring, the head, the fountain of your blood   **105**
 Is stopp'd; the very source of it is stopp'd.

MACDUFF Your royal father's murder'd.

MALCOLM O, by whom?

LENNOX [7] Those of his chamber, as it seem'd, had done't:

---

1 An image of the Day of Judgement. Another way of stressing the horror of the death of Duncan.

2 A nice irony, that the woman who has collaborated in the murder would collapse on hearing about it. In fact, Lady Macbeth does faint within the next fifty lines, but her collapse is probably a well-timed piece of acting to divert attention from Macbeth's increasingly bad performance.

3 human life

4 triviality

5 the dregs left at the bottom of a wine barrel or bottle

6 earth - the area under the 'vault' of heaven. This speech is ironic in that while pretending to convey Macbeth's assumed feelings on discovering the death of Duncan, it most probably expresses his true reaction ('Wake Duncan with thy knocking, I would thou couldst' - Act II, sc. ii, 86).

7 Lady Macbeth's prediction of court suspicions has proved correct

Their hands and faces were all badg'd with blood;   110
So were their daggers, which, unwip'd, we found
Upon their pillows:
They star'd, and were distracted; no man's life
Was to be trusted with them.

MACBETH O, yet I do repent me of my fury,   115
(1) That I did kill them.

MACDUFF Wherefore did you so?

MACBETH Who can be wise, amaz'd, temperate, and furious,
Loyal and neutral, in a moment? No man:
The expedition of my violent love   120
Out-ran the pauser reason. Here lay Duncan,
(2) His silver skin lac'd with his golden blood;
And his gash'd stabs look'd like a breach in nature
For ruin's wasteful entrance: there, the murderers,
Steep'd in the colours of their trade, their daggers   125
(3) Unmannerly breech'd with gore: who could refrain,
That had a heart to love, and in that heart
Courage to make's love known?

LADY MACBETH   Help me hence, ho!

MACDUFF Look to the lady.   130

MALCOLM   Why do we hold our tongues,
That most may claim this argument for ours?

DONALBAIN What should be spoken here, where our fate,
Hid in an (4) auger-hole, may rush, and seize us?
Let's away;   135
Our tears are not yet brew'd.

MALCOLM   Nor our strong sorrow
(5) Upon the foot of motion.

BANQUO   Look to the lady: –
    (LADY MACBETH *is carried out.*
And when we have our (6) naked frailties hid,   140
That suffer in exposure, let us meet,
And question this most bloody piece of work,
To know it further. Fears and scruples shake us:
In the great hand of God I stand; and, thence,
Against the undivulg'd pretence I fight   145
Of treasonous malice.

MACDUFF   And so do I.

ALL   So all.

MACBETH Let's briefly put on manly readiness
And meet i' the hall together.   150

---

1 Why, and when? His explanation is as questionable as the action itself, and suggests an unforeseen panic at the possibility of discovery. Thus, it is the first of a series of killings undertaken to cover up the truth.

2 This bizarre but beautiful description seems to be the product of Macbeth's awe of kingship, and horror at its destruction.

3 covered or clothed in blood, and therefore unmannerly, because convention would demand that the blades be sheathed. Perhaps too, an implication that unmannerly = unnatural.

4 a drill hole

5 Nor is our great grief ready for action yet.

6 when we have clothed our bare and therefore vulnerable bodies

ALL   Well contented.

                                  Exeunt all but MALCOLM *and* DONALBAIN.

MALCOLM What will you do? Let's not consort with them:
      To show an unfelt sorrow is an office
      Which the false man does easy. I'll to England.

DONALBAIN To Ireland I; our separated fortune   155
      Shall keep us both the safer: where we are,
      There's daggers in men's smiles: the *(1)* near' in blood,
      The nearer bloody.

MALCOLM   This murderous shaft that's shot
      Hath not yet lighted; and our safest way   160
      Is to avoid the aim. Therefore to horse;
      And let us not be dainty of leave-taking,
      But shift away: *(2)* there's warrant in that theft
      Which steals itself, when there's no mercy left.

                                                    Exeunt.

ACT TWO, SCENE FOUR
THE SAME – WITHOUT THE CASTLE

Enter ROSS, *and an* Old Man.

OLD MAN Threescore and ten I can remember well:
      Within the volume of which time I have seen
      Hours dreadful and things strange; but this sore night
      Hath trifled former knowings.

ROSS   Ah, good father,   5
      Thou seest, the heavens, as troubled with man's act,
      Threaten his *(3)* bloody stage: by the clock, 'tis day,
      And yet dark night strangles the travelling lamp;
      Is't night's predominance, or the day's shame,
      That *(4)* darkness does the face of earth entomb,   10
      When living light should kiss it?

OLD MAN   'Tis unnatural,
      Even like the deed that's done. On Tuesday last,
      A falcon, towering in her pride of place,
      Was by a mousing owl hawk'd at and kill'd.   15

ROSS And Duncan's horses. – a thing most strange and certain, –
      Beauteous and swift, the *(5)* minions of their race,
      Turn'd wild in nature, broke their stalls, flung out,
      (6) Contending 'gainst obedience, as they would make

1 the nearer we are by
     relationship to Duncan,
     the more likely we are to
     be victims ourselves

2 it is justifiable to steal
     away oneself when there
     is no apparent mercy to
     be hoped for

3 earth (another Playhouse
     image, like the famous
     one in Act V, sc. v)

4 This whole speech is
     dense with suggestions of
     profound evil; 'strangle',
     'shame', and 'entomb'
     combine to form an
     image of violence and
     death which is tragically
     contrasted by the
     nostalgia of 'when living
     light should kiss it'.

5 darlings of their kind
     These omens are all of
     unnatural behaviour, the
     result of the moral
     confusion created by evil.

6 rebelling against their
     obedience to man, as if
     they would make war on
     the human race

War with mankind.   20

OLD MAN   'Tis said they eat each other.

ROSS They did so; to the amazement of mine eyes,

That look'd upon't. Here comes the good Macduff.

Enter MACDUFF

How goes the world, sir, now?

MACDUFF   Why, see you not?   25

ROSS Is't known who did this more than bloody deed?

MACDUFF Those that Macbeth hath slain.

ROSS   Alas, the day!

What good could they pretend?

MACDUFF   They were *(1)* suborn'd: 30

Malcolm and Donalbain, the king's two sons,

Are stol'n away and fled; which puts upon them

Suspicion of the deed.

ROSS   'Gainst nature still:

Thriftless ambition, that wilt *(2)* ravin up   35

Thine own life's means! – Then 'tis most like,

The sovereignty will fall upon Macbeth.

MACDUFF He is already nam'd; and gone to *(3)* Scone

To be invested.

ROSS   Where is Duncan's body?   40

MACDUFF Carried to *(4)* Colme-kill,

The sacred storehouse of his predecessors,

The guardian of their bones.

ROSS   Will you to Scone?

MACDUFF No, cousin, I'll to Fife.   45

ROSS   Well, I will thither.

MACDUFF Well, may you see things well done there, – adieu! –

(5) Lest our old robes sit easier than our new!

ROSS Farewell, father.

OLD MAN God's benison go with you; and with those   50

That would make good of bad, and friends of foes!   *Exeunt.*

1 persuaded by someone else to do an evil deed

2 devour - a comment very apposite to Macbeth's own case

3 Scone was the ancient royal city north of Perth, originally the site of the 'Stone of Scone' on which the early kings of Scotland were crowned.

4 Colme-kill was another name for Iona, traditional burial place of Scotland's kings.

5 in case this new reign proves less comfortable for us than its predecessor

ACT THREE, SCENE ONE
FORRES – A ROOM IN THE PALACE

Enter BANQUO.

BANQUO Thou hast it now, – king, Cawdor, Glamis, all
    As the weird women promis'd; and, I fear,
    Thou play'dst most foully for't: yet it was said
    It should not stand in thy posterity;
    But that *(1)* myself should be the root and father   5
    Of many kings. If there come truth from them, –
    As upon thee, Macbeth, their speeches shine, –
    Why, by the *(2)* verities on thee made good,
    May they not be my oracles as well,
    And *(3)* set me up in hope? But, hush; no more.   10

Sennet sounded. Enter MACBETH *as King.*
LADY MACBETH *as Queen;* LENNOX, ROSS,
Lords, Ladies, *and* Attendants.
MACBETH Here's our chief guest.
LADY MACBETH   If he had been forgotten,
    It had been as a gap in our great feast,
    And *(4)* all-thing unbecoming.
MACBETH To-night we hold a solemn supper, sir,   15
    And I'll request your presence.
BANQUO   Let your highness
    Command upon me; to the which my duties
    Are with a most indissoluble tie
    For ever knit.   20
MACBETH Ride you this afternoon?
BANQUO   Ay, my good lord.
MACBETH We should have else desir'd your good advice, –
    Which *(5)* still hath been both grave and prosperous,
    In this day's council; but we'll take to-morrow.   25
    Is't far you ride?
BANQUO As far, my lord, as will fill up the time
    'Twixt this and supper: go not my horse the better,
    (6) I must become a borrower of the night,
    For a dark hour or twain.   30
MACBETH   Fail not our feast.
BANQUO My lord, I will not.
MACBETH We hear our bloody cousins are bestow'd

1 Banquo reflects on the Witches' promise to him that his children should be kings, but clearly has no intention of trying to bring this about. His suspicions of Macbeth are very strong now.

2 truths

3 give me hope for the future

4 totally improper

5 always

6 An ironic interchange; Banquo's 'dark night' will be eternal

In England and in Ireland; not confessing
Their cruel *(1)* parricide, filling their hearers   35   *1   murder of a father*
With strange invention: but of that to-morrow;
When therewithal we shall have cause of state
Craving us jointly. Hie you to horse: adieu,
Till you return at night. Goes Fleance with you?

BANQUO Ay, my good lord: our time does call upon's.   40

MACBETH I wish your horses swift and sure of foot;
And so I do commend you to their backs.
Farewell. –   *Exit* BANQUO.
Let every man be master of his time
Till seven at night; to make society   45
The sweeter welcome, we will keep ourself
Till supper-time alone: while then, God be with you!
                    (Exeunt LADY MACBETH, Lords, Ladies, & c.
Sirrah, a word with you: attend those men
Our pleasure?

ATTENDANT They are, my lord, without the palace gate.   50

MACBETH Bring them before us.   *Exit* Attendant.
                        (2) To be thus is nothing;   *2   we have gained nothing*
But to be safely thus: – our fears in Banquo   *unless we can be sure in*
Stick deep: and in his royalty of nature   *our position*
Reigns that which would be fear'd: 'tis much he dares;   55
And, to that dauntless temper of his mind,
He hath a wisdom that doth guide his valour
To act in safety. There is none but he
Whose being I do fear: and, under him,
My *(3)* genius is rebuk'd; as, it is said,   60   *3   guardian angel or spirit*
Mark Antony's was by Cæsar. He chid the sisters   *4   fruitless because it would*
When first they put the name of king upon me,   *not be handed down to*
And bade them speak to him; then, prophet-like,   *his children*
They hail'd him father to a line of kings: *5   unrelated*
Upon my head they plac'd a *(4)* fruitless crown,   65   *6   defiled, corrupted*
And put a barren sceptre in my gripe,   *7   embittered my peace of*
Thence to be wrench'd with an *(5)* unlineal hand,   *mind. Macbeth's use of*
No son of mine succeeding. If't be so,   *the image of a 'vessel' of*
For Banquo's issue have I *(6)* fil'd my mind;   *peace recalls his earlier*
For them the gracious Duncan have I murder'd;   70   *'our poisoned chalice';*
Put *(7)* rancours in the vessel of my peace   *both seem to include the*
Only for them; and *(8)* mine eternal jewel   *subconscious recognition*
Given to the common enemy of man,   *of personal responsibility.*
To make them kings, the seed of Banquo kings!   *8   my soul*

(1) Rather than so, come, fate, into the list,   75
And champion me to the utterance! – Who's there? –

Re-enter Attendant, *with two* Murderers
Now go to the door, and stay there till we call.

                                Exit Attendant.
Was it not yesterday we spoke together?

1 MURDERER It was, so please your highness.

MACBETH   Well then, now   80
Have you consider'd of my speeches? Know
That *(2)* it was he, in the times past, which held you
So under fortune; which you thought had been
Our innocent self: this I made good to you
In our last conference, *(3)* pass'd in probation with you,   85
How you were *(4)* borne in hand, how cross'd, the instruments,
Who wrought with them, and all things else that might
To half a soul and to a notion craz'd
Say, *Thus did Banquo.*

1 MURDERER   You made it known to us.   90

MACBETH I did so; and went further, which is now
Our point of second meeting. Do you find
Your patience so predominant in your nature,
That you can let this go? Are you so *(5)* gospell'd,
To pray for this good man and for his issue,   95
Whose heavy hand hath bow'd you to the grave,
And beggar'd yours for ever?

1 MURDERER   We are men, my liege.

MACBETH Ay, in the catalogue ye go for men;
As hounds, and greyhounds, mongrels, spaniels, curs,   100
(6) Shoughs, water-rugs, and demi-wolves are clept
All by the name of dogs: the *(7)* valu'd file
Distinguishes the swift, the slow, the subtle,
The house-keeper, the hunter, every one
According to the gift which bounteous nature   105
Hath in him clos'd; whereby he does receive
(8) Particular addition, from the bill
That writes them all alike: and so of men.
Now, if you have a station in the file,
And not i' the worst rank of manhood, say it;   110
And I will put that business in your bosoms,
Whose execution *(9)* takes your enemy off;
Grapples you to the heart and love of us,

1   To avoid this, let Fate be my champion to the bitter end. He means to defy the prophecy by killing Fleance.

2   Macbeth now systematically deceives the hired cut-throats into believing Banquo their long-time enemy. His ability to plot and execute coolly shows how far he has moved from his state of mind before Duncan's murder. Despite the apparent speed of the action of the plot, we have here a sense that some time has elapsed.

3   explained the proof to you

4   deceived by false appearances

5   so forgivingly Christian as to . . .

6   shaggy-haired dogs, rough-coated water dogs and cross-breeds, all called 'dogs'. By the comparison with dogs, Macbeth is taunting the men to prove their manly 'courage', by revenge and murder. Lady Macbeth's taunting of him in Act I, sc. vii is recalled here.

7   list of values or prices

8   a special quality

9   removes, kills Banquo, your foe

Who wear our health but sickly in his life,
(1) Which in his death were perfect.   115

2 MURDERER   I am one, my liege,
Whom the vile blows and buffets of the world
Have so incens'd that I am reckless what
I do to spite the world.

1 MURDERER   And I another,   120
So weary with disasters, tugg'd with fortune
That I would set my life on any chance,
To mend it, or be rid on't.

MACBETH   Both of you
Know Banquo was your enemy.   125

BOTH MURDERERS True, my lord.

MACBETH So is he mine; and in such bloody distance,
That every minute of his being *(2)* thrusts
Against my near'st of life: and though I could
With bare-fac'd power sweep him from my sight,   130
And *(3)* bid my will avouch it, yet I must not,
For certain friends that are both his and mine,
Whose loves I may not drop, but wail his fall
Who I myself struck down: and thence it is
That I to your assistance do make love;   135
Masking the business from the common eye
For sundry weighty reasons.

2 MURDERER   We shall, my lord,
Perform what you command us.

1 MURDERER   Though our lives –   140

MACBETH Your spirits shine through you. Within this
        hour at most,
I will advise you where to plant yourselves;
Acquaint you with the *(4)* perfect spy o' the time,
The moment on't; for't must be done to-night,   145
And *(5)* something from the palace; always thought
That *(6)* I require a clearness: and with him, –
To leave no rubs nor botches in the work, –
Fleance his son, that keeps him company,
Whose absence is no less material to me   150
Than is his father's, must embrace the fate
Of that dark hour. Resolve yourselves apart:
I'll come to you anon.

BOTH MURDERERS   We are resolv'd, my lord.

MACBETH I'll call upon you straight: abide within.   155

---

1 Macbeth's assumption that, with Banquo removed, his problems will be over, is both naive and ironic. Note his use of the 'royal we', as often when he is striving to impress.

2 threatens my very heart

3 . . . and justify it as my desire, simply. . .

4 the best opportunity. Several editors have taken this to mean the introduction of another murderer, and linked it with the appearance of the third cut-throat at the scene of the crime, but 'spy' can mean 'espial'

5 well away from

6 I need to be above suspicion, to have an alibi

Exeunt Murderers.

It is concluded: – Banquo, thy soul's flight,
If it find heaven, must find it out to-night.   *Exit.*

ACT THREE, SCENE TWO
THE SAME – ANOTHER ROOM IN THE PALACE

Enter LADY MACBETH, *and a* Servant.

LADY MACBETH Is Banquo gone from court?

SERVANT Ay, madam, but returns again to-night.

LADY MACBETH *(1)* Say to the king, I would attend his leisure
    For a few words.

SERVANT   Madam, I will.   *Exit.*   5

LADY MACBETH *(2)* Naught's had, all's spent,
    Where our desire is got without content:
    'Tis safer to be that which we destroy,
    Than, by destruction, dwell in doubtful joy.

Enter MACBETH.

    How now, my lord! why do you keep alone,   10
    Of sorriest fancies your companions making;
    Using those thoughts which should indeed have died
    With them they think on? Things without all remedy
    Should be without regard: what's done is done.

MACBETH We have *(3)* scotch'd the snake, not kill'd it;   15
    She'll *(4)* close, and be herself; whilst our poor malice
    Remains in danger of her former tooth.
    But let the frame of things disjoint,
    Both the worlds suffer,
    (5) Ere we will eat our meal in fear, and sleep   20
    In the affliction of these terrible dreams
    That shake us nightly: better be with the dead,
    Whom we, to gain our peace, have sent to peace,
    Than *(6)* on the torture of the mind to lie
    In restless ecstacy. Duncan is in his grave;   25
    After life's fitful fever he sleeps well;
    Treason had done his worst: nor steel, nor poison,
    Malice domestic, foreign levy, nothing
    Can touch him further.

LADY MACBETH   Come on;   30

---

1 The distance between Lady Macbeth and her husband now is clear; she has to sue for a few moments of his time.

2 'Nothing is gained, everything is wasted'. Lady Macbeth echoes Macbeth's thoughts of the previous scene ('to be thus is nothing, but to be safely thus'), but, concerned for his state of mind, conceals her own on his entry.

3 gashed, wounded

4 heal

5 these lines are proof of the continuing guilt and anguish that he is suffering

6 The image here is of the rack, an instrument of torture on which the body was stretched to snapping point in order to gain information. 'Ecstacy' means agony.

Gentle my lord, sleek o'er your rugged looks:
Be bright and jovial 'mong your guests to-night.
MACBETH So shall I, love; and so, I pray, be you:
Let your remembrance apply to Banquo;
[1] Present him eminence, both with eye and tongue: 35
Unsafe the while, that we
Must [2] lave our honours in these flattering streams:
And make our faces [3] vizards to our hearts,
Disguising what they are.
LADY MACBETH   You must leave this.   40
MACBETH O, full of scorpions is my mind, dear wife!
Thou know'st that Banquo, and his Fleance, lives.
LADY MACBETH But in them [4] nature's copy's not eterne.
MACBETH There's comfort yet; they are assailable;
Then be thou jocund: ere the bat hath flown   45
His cloister'd flight; ere, to black Hecate's summons,
The [5] shard-borne beetle, with his drowsy hums,
Hath rung night's yawning peal, there shall be done
A deed of dreadful note.
LADY MACBETH   What's to be done?   50
MACBETH Be [6] innocent of the knowledge, dearest chuck,
Till thou applaud the deed. Come, [7] seeling night,
Scarf up the tender eye of pitiful day;
And with thy bloody and invisible hand
Cancel and tear to pieces that great [8] bond   55
Which keeps me pale! – Light thickens; and the crow
Makes wing to the rooky wood:
Good things of day begin to droop and drowse;
Whiles night's black agents to their prey do rouse. –
Thou marvell'st at my words: but hold thee still;   60
Things bad begun make strong themselves by ill:
So, pr'ythee, go with me.   *Exeunt.*

ACT THREE, SCENE THREE

THE SAME — A PARK OR LAWN, WITH A GATE LEADING TO THE PALACE

Enter three Murderers.

1 MURDERER But who did bid thee join with us?
3 MURDERER   Macbeth.
2 MURDERER He needs not our mistrust: since [9] he delivers

1 give him special (V.I.P.)
   treatment
2 keep clean, preserve
3 masks - another image of
   the deceiving face
4 their lease of life is not
   forever
5 'carried on scaly wings'
   Macbeth's use of
   the singularly
   inappropriate word
   'jocund', and his
   melodramatic secrecy,
   strike a chilling note.
6 The distance between the
   two is enhanced by his
   use of the familiar
   'dearest chuck' when he
   is actually forbidding her
   knowledge of his plans.
   He needs the re-
   assurance of her applause
   for a deed he has
   organised without her.
7 'blinding' - an image
   taken from hawking,
   where the hawk's eyes
   were 'seeled' by being
   sewn up to prevent it
   seeing in training
8 the natural law binding
   mankind together and
   forbidding murder
   Macbeth's invocation of
   darkness equals, if it does
   not outdo, his wife's
   (Act I, sc. v, 51). He
   seems more concerned
   with avoiding 'tenderness
   and pity', she with the
   intervention of heaven;
   both evoke the opacity of
   darkness in her 'blanket
   of the dark' and his 'light
   thickens'.
9 informs us of our duties
   according to his specific
   instructions

Our offices, and what we have to do,
To the direction just.   5

1 MURDERER   Then stand with us.
The west yet glimmers with some streaks of day:
Now spurs the [1] lated traveller apace,   *1 delayed*
To gain the timely inn; and near approaches
The subject of our watch.   10

3 MURDERER   Hark! I hear horses.

BANQUO *(Within.)* Give us a light there, ho!

2 MURDERER   Then 'tis he; the rest
That are [2] within the note of expectation   *2 expected guests*
Already are i' the court.   15

1 MURDERER   His horses go about.

3 MURDERER Almost a mile; but he does usually,
So all men do, from hence to the palace gate
Make it their walk.

2 MURDERER   A light, a light!   20

3 MURDERER   'Tis he.

1 MURDERER Stand to't.

Enter BANQUO, *and* FLEANCE *with a torch.*

BANQUO It will be rain to-night.

1 MURDERER   [3] Let it come down.*(Assaults* BANQUO.   *3 a grim pun - 'let it rain*

BANQUO O treachery! Fly, good Fleance, fly, fly, fly!   25   *blows upon his head'*
Thou mayst revenge. – O slave!   *(Dies.* FLEANCE *escapes.*

3 MURDERER Who did strike out the light?

1 MURDERER   [4] Was't not the way?   *4 Was it not the best thing*

3 MURDERER There's but one down: the son is fled.   *to do?*

2 MURDERER We have lost best half of our affair.   30

1 MURDERER Well, let's away, and say how much is done.   *Exeunt.*

ACT THREE, SCENE FOUR

THE SAME – A ROOM OF STATE IN THE PALACE. A BANQUET PREPARED

Enter MACBETH, LADY MACBETH, ROSS, LENNOX, Lords *and*
Attendants.

MACBETH You know your own [5] degrees, sit down: as first   *5 ranks*
And last the hearty welcome.   *6 Macbeth plays the king*

LORDS   Thanks to your majesty.   *here, self-consciously*

MACBETH [6] Ourself will mingle with society,   *using the 'royal we'.*

And play the humble host.   **5**

Our hostess *(1)* keeps her state; but, in best time,

We will require her welcome.

LADY MACBETH Pronounce it for me, sir, to all our friends;

For my heart speaks they are welcome.

MACBETH See, they encounter thee with their hearts' thanks. –   **10**

Both sides are even: here I'll sit i' the midst:

Enter first Murderer *to the door.*

Be *(2)* large in mirth; anon we'll drink a measure

The table round. – There's blood upon thy face.

MURDERER 'Tis Banquo's then.

MACBETH 'Tis better thee without than he within.   **15**

Is he *(3)* despatch'd?

MURDERER My lord, his throat is cut; that I did for him.

MACBETH Thou art the best o' the cut-throats:

Yet he's good that did the like for Fleance.

If thou didst it, thou art the *(4)* nonpareil.   **20**

MURDERER   Most royal, sir,

Fleance is 'scap'd.

MACBETH Then comes my fit again: I had else been perfect;

Whole as the marble, founded as the rock;

(5) As broad and general as the casing air: **25**

But now I am cabin'd, cribb'd, confin'd, bound in

To *(6)* saucy doubts and fears. But Banquo's safe?

MURDERER Ay, my good lord: safe in a ditch he bides,

With *(7)* twenty trenched gashes on his head;

The least a death to nature.   **30**

MACBETH   Thanks for that:

There the *(8)* grown serpent lies; the worm that's fled

Hath nature that in time will venom breed,

No teeth for the present. – Get thee gone; to-morrow

We'll hear, ourselves, again.   *Exit* Murderer. **35**

LADY MACBETH   My royal lord,

You do not give the cheer: the feast is sold

That is not often vouch'd, while 'tis a-making,

'Tis given with welcome: *(9)* to feed were best at home

From thence the sauce to meat is ceremony;   **40**

Meeting were bare without it.

MACBETH   Sweet remembrancer! –

Now, good digestion wait on appetite,

And health on both!

---

1 remains in her chair of state

2 relax and be convivial

3 killed

4 incomparable

5 as free and easy as the air around us - the idea of 'casing' is picked up in the claustrophobic metaphors 'cabin'd, cribb'd, confined, bound in', which convey the stifling effect of his terror

6 hostile

7 twenty cuts hacked in his head, the smallest enough to kill him

8 Banquo, the grown serpent, is no longer a fear; but Fleance, the 'worm' who will grow to manhood, means danger for the future.

9 if we feast away from home, the occasion demands ceremony to make it special

LENNOX	May't please your highness sit?	45

(The Ghost of BANQUO *rises, and sits in* MACBETH'S *place.*

MACBETH [1] Here had we now our country's honour roof'd,
    Were the grac'd person of our Banquo present;
    Who may I rather challenge for unkindness
    Than pity for mischance!

ROSS His absence, sir.   50
    Lays blame upon his promise. Please't your highness
    To grace us with your royal company.

MACBETH The table's full.

LENNOX Here's a place reserv'd, sir.

MACBETH Where?   55

LENNOX Here, my lord. What is't that moves your highness?

MACBETH Which of you have done this?

LORDS What, my good lord?

MACBETH Thou canst not say I did it: never shake
    Thy gory locks at me.   60

ROSS Gentlemen, rise; his highness is not well.

LADY MACBETH Sit, worthy friends: – my lord is often thus,
    And hath been from his youth: pray you, keep seat.
    The fit is momentary; upon a thought
    He will again be well: if much you note him   65
    You shall offend him, and extend his passion:
    Feed, and regard him not. – Are you a man?

MACBETH Ay, and a bold one, that dare look on that
    Which might appal the devil.

LADY MACBETH O proper stuff!   70
    [2] This is the very painting of your fear:
    This is the air-drawn dagger which, you said,
    Led you to Duncan. O, [3] these flaws, and starts, –
    Impostors to true fear, – would well become
    A woman's story at a winter's fire,   75
    [4] Authoriz'd by her grandam. Shame itself!
    Why do you make such faces? When all's done,
    You look but on a stool.

MACBETH Pr'ythee, see there!
    Behold! look! lo! how say you? –   80
    Why, what care I? If thou canst nod, speak
    If [5] charnel-houses and our graves must send
    Those that we bury back, our [6] monuments
    Shall be the maws of kites.   (Ghost *disappears.*

LADY MACBETH What, quite unmann'd in folly?   85

---

1   'If Banquo were here, we would have the most distinguished noblemen of Scotland under our roof; I hope his failure to appear is merely ungraciousness, and not the result of accident'. An ironically cool statement, almost immediately contrasted by his terror at the apparition.

2   'This is an image created by your terror, like the imagined dagger.'

3   outbursts

4   'a positive granny's story' Here again Lady Macbeth implies effeminacy by her choice of words, knowing its power to rouse Macbeth's courage.

5   vaults for the dead

6   'our tombs will be the bellies of predatory birds'

41

MACBETH If I stand here, I saw him.

LADY MACBETH   Fie, for shame!

MACBETH Blood hath been shed ere now, i' the olden time,
    Ere [1] human statute purg'd the gentle weal;
    Ay, and since too, murders have been perform'd   90
    Too terrible for the ear: the times have been,
    That, when the brains were out, the man would die,
    And there an end; but now they rise again,
    With [2] twenty mortal murders on their crowns,
    And push us from our stools: this is more strange   95
    Than such a murder is.

LADY MACBETH   My worthy lord,
    Your noble friends do lack you.

MACBETH   I do forget: –
    Do not muse at me, my most worthy friends;   100
    I have a strange infirmity, which is nothing
    To those that know me. Come, love and health to all;
    Then I'll sit down. – Give me some wine, fill full.
    I drink to the general joy o' the whole table,
    And to our dear friend Banquo, whom we miss;   105
    Would he were here! to all, and him, we thirst,
    And all to all.

LORDS   Our duties, and the pledge.

                    (Ghost *rises again.*

MACBETH Avaunt! and quit my sight! let the earth hide thee!
    Thy bones are marrowless, thy blood is cold;   110
    Thou hast no [3] speculation in those eyes
    Which thou dost glare with!

LADY MACBETH   Think of this, good peers,
    But as a [4] thing of custom: 'tis no other;
    Only it spoils the pleasure of the time.   115

MACBETH What man dare, I dare:
    Approach thou like the rugged Russian bear,
    The [5] arm'd rhinoceros, or the [6] Hyrcan tiger;
    Take any shape but that, and my firm nerves
    Shall never tremble: or be alive again,   120
    And dare me to the desert with thy sword;
    [7] If trembling I inhabit then, protest me
    The baby of a girl. Hence, horrible shadow!
    Unreal mockery, hence!   (Ghost *disappears.*
             Why, so; – being gone,   125
    I am a man again. – Pray you, sit still.

1 before the state was
    civilised by humane laws

2 twenty fatal gashes on
    their heads. He finds the
    return of the dead
    horrifyingly unnatural but
    fails to perceive, of
    course, that his own
    murder of innocence
    partakes of the same
    unnatural quality

3 intelligence

4 a habitual action

5 armoured, protected

6 Hyrcania was a Persian
    province, said to be the
    breeding ground for
    tigers

7 Macbeth protests his
    courage is strong for
    anything but the sight of
    the bloody Banquo.
    Indeed it has been proved
    in single combat with
    Macdonwald (Act I, sc. ii,
    11), and will be again
    with Macduff (Act V,
    sc. viii, 10)

LADY MACBETH You have displac'd the mirth, broke the good meeting,
   With most *(1)* admir'd disorder.
MACBETH   Can such things be,
   And overcome us like a summer's cloud.   130
   Without our special wonder? *(2)* You make me strange
   Even to the disposition that I owe,
   When now I think you can behold such sights,
   And keep the natural ruby of your cheeks,
   When mine are blanch'd with fear.   135
ROSS   What sights, my lord?
LADY MACBETH I pray you, speak not; he grows worse and worse;
   Question enrages him: at once, good-night: –
   (3) Stand not upon the order of your going,
   But go at once.   140
LENNOX   Good-night; and better health
   Attend his majesty!
LADY MACBETH   A kind good-night to all!
                              Exeunt Lords *and* Attendants.
MACBETH It will have blood; they say, blood will have blood:
   Stones have been known to move, and trees to speak;   145
   (4) Augurs, and understood relations, have
   By *(5)* magot-pies, and choughs, and rooks, brought forth
   The secret'st man of blood. – What is the night?
LADY MACBETH Almost at odds with morning, which is which.
MACBETH How say'st thou, that *(6)* Macduff denies his person,   150
   At our great bidding?
LADY MACBETH   Did you send to him, sir?
MACBETH I hear it by the way; but I will send:
   There's not a one of them, but in his house
   I keep a servant *(7)* fee'd. *(8)* I will to-morrow   155
   (And betimes I will) to the weird sisters:
   More shall they speak; for now I am bent to know,
   By the worst means, the worst. For mine own good,
   (9) All causes shall give way: I am in blood
   Stept in so far that, should I wade no more,   160
   Returning were as tedious as go o'er:
   (10) Strange things I have in head, that will to hand;
   Which must be acted ere they may be scann'd.
LADY MACBETH You lack the season of all natures, sleep.
MACBETH Come, we'll to sleep. My strange and self-abuse   165
   (11) Is the initiate fear, that wants hard use: –
   We are yet but young in deed.   *Exeunt.*

1 amazing
2 You force me to be unlike myself. (Macbeth thinks that Lady Macbeth can see Banquo's ghost, and cannot comprehend her cool reaction to it.)
3 Do not delay by leaving in order of rank.
4 prophecies and interpretations of the unusual habits of birds have exposed guilty deeds. The panic of his guilt is vividly evoked by the repetition of the word blood in line 144.
5 magpies and jackdaws
6 The movement of Macbeth's thoughts is dramatically clear; his fears, now that Banquo has been removed, centre on Macduff.
7 in my pay - this again suggests that some time has elapsed
8 This decisiveness marks another downward step - he needs the support of the forces of evil (for the first time, apparently). His resolution and bravado are chilling.
9 Irony. He still perceives evil as the way to his own good. He sees that his progress in blood is inevitable, but not what the outcome must be.
10 I shall put my policies into action first, and assess them afterwards. (A clear avoidance of moral responsibility, now.)
11 My delusions are simply the product of a beginner's fear; I need greater experience of evil deeds.

ACT THREE, SCENE FIVE
THE HEATH

(1) Thunder. Enter the three Witches, *meeting* HECATE.

1 WITCH Why, how now, Hecate! you look angerly.
HECATE Have I not reason, *(2)* beldams as you are,
    Saucy and overbold? How did you dare
    To trade and traffic with Macbeth
    In riddles and affairs of death;   5
    And I, the mistress of your charms,
    The close contriver of all harms,
    Was never call'd to bear my part,
    Or show the glory of our art?
    And, which is worse, all you have done   10
    Hath been but for a wayward son,
    Spiteful and wrathful; who, as others do,
    Loves for his own ends, not for you.
    But make amends now: get you gone,
    And at the pit of *(3)* Acheron   15
    Meet me i' the morning: thither he
    Will come to know his destiny.
    Your vessels and your spells provide,
    Your charms, and everything beside.
    I am for the air: this night I'll spend   20
    Unto a dismal and a fatal end.
    Great business must be wrought ere noon:
    Upon the corner of the moon
    There hangs a vaporous drop profound;
    I'll catch it ere it come to ground: 25
    And that, distill'd by magic sleights,
    Shall raise such *(4)* artificial sprites,
    As, by the strength of their illusion,
    Shall draw him on to his confusion:
    He shall spurn fate, scorn death, and bear   30
    His hopes 'bove wisdom, grace, and fear:
    (5) And you all know, security
    Is mortal's chiefest enemy.
            (Music and song within: (6) Come away, come away. & c.
    Hark! I am call'd; my little spirit, see,
    Sits in a foggy cloud, and stays for me.   *Exit.*   35
1 WITCH Come, let's make haste; she'll soon be back again.   *Exeunt.*

---

1 This scene is thought not to be by Shakespeare, but to be a contemporary interpolation. With the exception of the end of Hecate's speech, it has little dramatic relevance, lacks focus, and is undistinguished in the writing.

2 hags

3 Acheron is one of the rivers of the underworld, used here of Hell.

4 e.g. the Apparitions, as seen in Act IV, sc. i.

5 Hecate stresses Macbeth's hope for the future as a chief motive, and points out that because he needs to feel secure, he can easily be given the illusion of security. This is exactly the psychology of the Apparitions; a superficial response gives Macbeth a sense of safety, where a more searching analysis of their meaning would have indicated a contrary reaction.

6 This song, and that in Act IV, sc i, are thought to be additions from Middleton's "The Witch".

44

ACT THREE, SCENE SIX
A ROOM IN THE PALACE

Enter LENNOX, *and another* Lord.

LENNOX My former speeches have but *(1)* hit your thoughts,
    Which can interpret further: only, I say,
    Things have been *(2)* strangely borne. The gracious Duncan
    Was pitied of Macbeth: – marry, he was dead: –
    And the right-valiant Banquo walk'd too late;   5
    Whom, you may say, if't please you, Fleance kill'd,
    For Fleance fled. Men must not walk too late.
    Who cannot want the thought, how monstrous
    It was for Malcolm and for Donalbain
    To kill their gracious father? damned fact!   10
    How it did grieve Macbeth! did he not straight,
    In pious rage, the two delinquents tear,
    That were the slaves of drink and thralls of sleep?
    Was not that nobly done? Ay, and wisely too;
    For 'twould have anger'd any heart alive,   15
    To hear the men deny't. So that, I say,
    He has borne all things well: and I do think,
    That had he Duncan's sons under his key, –
    As, an't please Heaven, he shall not, – they should find
    What 'twere to kill a father; so should Fleance.   20
    But, peace! – for from *(3)* broad words, and 'cause he fail'd
    His presence at the tyrant's feast, I hear,
    Macduff lives in disgrace. Sir, can you tell
    Where he bestows himself?
LORD   The son of Duncan,   25
    From whom this *(4)* tyrant holds the due of birth,
    Lives in the English court; and is receiv'd
    Of the most pious Edward with such grace
    That the malevolence of fortune nothing
    Takes from his high respect: thither Macduff   30
    Is gone *(5)* to pray the holy king, upon his aid
    To wake Northumberland, and warlike Siward:
    That, by the help of these, – with Him above
    To ratify the work, – we may again
    Give to our tables meat, sleep to our nights;   35
    Free from our feasts and banquets bloody knives;
    Do faithful homage, and receive free honours, –

1 What I have said is just suggestion, for your own further thought. Lennox's speeches voice the growing suspicions of Macbeth throughout Scotland. The scene also makes clear that Macduff has fled to England, so that the audience sees Macbeth's growing optimism juxtaposed with a very threatening counter-movement.

2 curiously carried out

3 speaking his mind openly

4 References to Macbeth as tyrant and traitor proliferate; it has to be clear that to rebel against such a king is justifiable.

5 Edward the Confessor, introduced at this point, is made much of as a holy king, and therefore as the antithesis of Macbeth. He epitomises the ideal qualities of kingship and is, in addition, a healer. His aid to Malcolm brings healing to Scotland eventually, though it is by the sword, a radical operation to excise an evil, rather than the gentle prayers described by Malcolm in Act IV, sc. iii.

All which we pine for now: and this report
Hath so exasperate the king that he
Prepares for some attempt of war.   40
LENNOX   Sent he to Macduff?
LORD He did: and with an absolute *Sir, not I,*
The *(1)* cloudy messenger turns me his back,   *1 surly messenger*
And hums, as who should say, *You'll rue the time*
That *(2)* clogs me with this answer.   45   *2 burdens me*
LENNOX And that well might
Advise him to a caution, to hold what distance
His wisdom can provide. Some holy angel
Fly to the court of England, and unfold
His message ere he come; that a swift blessing   50
May soon return to this our suffering country
Under a hand accurs'd!
LORD   I'll send my prayers with him!   *Exeunt.*

ACT FOUR, SCENE ONE

A DARK CAVE – IN THE MIDDLE, A CAULDRON BOILING

Thunder. Enter the three Witches.
1 WITCH Thrice the *(3)* brinded cat hath mew'd.   *3 brindled*
2 WITCH Thrice; and once the hedge-pig whin'd.
3 WITCH *(4)* Harpier cries: – 'tis time, 'tis time.   *4 Harper/Harpier is*
1 WITCH Round about the cauldron go;   *probably a harpy, a*
In the poison'd entrails throw. –   5   *mythical creature of evil.*
Toad, that under cold stone,   *The cat and hedgehog are*
Days and nights has thirty-one   *familiars of the Witches.*
Swelter'd venom sleeping got,
Boil thou first i' the charmed pot!
ALL Double, double toil and trouble;   10
Fire, burn; and, cauldron, bubble.
2 WITCH Fillet of a fenny snake,
In the cauldron boil and bake;
Eye of newt, and toe of frog,
Wool of bat, and tongue of dog,   15
Adder's fork, and blind-worm's sting,
Lizard's leg, and howlet's wing, –
For a charm of powerful trouble,

Like a hell-broth boil and bubble.

ALL Double, double toil and trouble,   20

    Fire, burn; and, cauldron, bubble.

3 WITCH Scale of dragon, tooth of wolf,

    Witches' *(1)* mummy, maw and *(2)* gulf

    Of the *(3)* ravin'd salt-sea shark,

    Root of *(4)* hemlock digg'd i' the dark,   25

    Liver of blaspheming Jew,

    Gall of goat, and slips of yew

    (5) Sliver'd in the moon's eclipse,

    Nose of *(6)* Turk, and Tartar's lips,

    Finger of birth-strangl'd babe,   30

    Ditch-deliver'd by a *(7)* drab, –

    Make the gruel thick and *(8)* slab:

    Add thereto a tiger's *(9)* chaudron,

    For the ingredients of our cauldron.

ALL Double, double toil and trouble;   35

    Fire, burn; and, cauldron, bubble.

2 WITCH Cool it with a baboon's blood,

    Then the charm is firm and good.

Enter HECATE.

(10) **HECATE** O, well done! I commend your pains;

    And every one shall share i' the gains.   40

    And now about the cauldron sing,

    Like elves and fairies in a ring,

    Enchanting all that you put in.

                             (Music and a Song.

    Black spirits and white, red spirits and gray;

    Mingle, mingle, mingle, you that mingle may.   *Exit* HECATE.   45

2 WITCH By the pricking of my thumbs,

    Something wicked this way comes: –   *(Knocking.*

    Open, locks, whoever knocks!

Enter MACBETH

(11) **MACBETH** <u>How now, you secret, black, and midnight hags</u>!

    What is't you do!   50

ALL   A deed without a name.

MACBETH I conjure you, by that which you profess, –

    Howe'er you come to know it, – answer me:

    <u>Though you untie the winds, and let them fight</u>

    <u>Against the churches; though the *(12)* yesty waves</u>   55

1 a medical substance made from corpses, here of witches

2 stomach, gulping for food

3 ravenous, predatory

4 poisonous plant, made more deadly by being dug up at night

5 sliced off during the blackness of an eclipse

6 Turks and Tartars were non-Christian, like the 'blaspheming Jew' - hence, like the 'birth-strangled babe', they had not had the devil expelled from them by baptism. They were also renowned for savagery.

7 prostitute

8 solid

9 entrails

10 Hecate's lines, which lower the dramatic tension to the point of anti-climax, are certainly not in Shakespeare's text, and were presumably added to introduce the later addition of the second song from Middleton's "The Witch".

11 A moment of immense bravado! Macbeth's next speech proclaims his determination to use all knowledge gained from the Witches, while clearly accepting its evil origin.

12 foaming

Confound and swallow navigation up;
Though bladed corn be *(1)* lodg'd, and trees blown down;
Though castles topple on their warders' heads;
Though palaces and pyramids do slope
Their heads to their foundations; though the treasure   60
Of nature's *(2)* germen tumble altogether,
(3) Even till destruction sicken, – answer me
To what I ask you.

1 Witch   Speak.

2 Witch   Demand.   65

3 Witch   We'll answer.

1 Witch Say, if thou'dst rather hear it from our mouths,
Or from our masters?

Macbeth   Call 'em, let me see 'em.

1 Witch Pour in sow's blood, that hath eaten   70
Her nine *(4)* farrow; grease that's sweaten
From the murderer's gibbet throw
Into the flame.

All   Come, high or low;
Thyself and *(5)* office deftly show!   75

Thunder. An Apparition *of an armed Head rises.*

Macbeth Tell me, thou unknown power, –

1 Witch   He knows thy thought:
Hear his speech, but say thou naught.

Apparition Macbeth! Macbeth! Macbeth! beware Macduff;
Beware the Thane of Fife. – Dismiss me: – enough.   *(Descends.*   80

Macbeth Whate'er thou art, for thy good caution, thanks;
Thou hast *(6)* harp'd my fear aright: – but one word more, –

1 Witch He will not be commanded: here's another,
More potent than the first.

Thunder. An Apparition *of a bloody Child rises.*

Apparition Macbeth! Macbeth! Macbeth! –   85

Macbeth Had I three ears, I'd hear thee.

Apparition Be bloody, bold, and resolute; laugh to scorn
The power of man, for none of woman born
Shall harm Macbeth.   *(Descends.*

Macbeth *(7)* Then live, Macduff: what need I fear of thee?   90
But yet I'll make assurance double sure,
And take a *(8)* bond of fate: thou shalt not live;
That I may tell pale-hearted fear it lies,

---

1 laid flat

2 seeds

3 An image of total confusion leading to such barrenness that even destruction is sickened of itself.

4 litter

5 purpose, function

6 guessed, interpreted

7 Macbeth ironically misinterprets the Witches' ambiguous and therefore deceptive apparitions. He hears what he wants to hear only, failing to question what is *seen* in conjunction with what is heard.

8 hold fate to its promise by legal agreement

And sleep in spite of thunder. – What is this,

Thunder. An Apparition *of a Child crowned, with a tree in his
hand, rises.*

That rises like the issue of a king,   95
And wears upon his baby brow the *(1)* round
And top of sovereignty?

ALL Listen, but speak not to't.

APPARITION Be lion-mettled, proud; and take no care
Who chafes, who frets, or where conspirers are: 100
(2) Macbeth shall never vanquish'd be, until
Great Birnam wood to high Dunsinane hill
Shall come against him.   *(Descends.*

MACBETH   That will never be;
Who can *(3)* impress the forest; bid the tree   105
Unfix his earth-bound root? Sweet *(4)* bodements! good!
Rebellion's head, rise never, till the wood
Of Birnam rise, and our high-plac'd Macbeth
Shall live the *(5)* lease of nature, pay his breath
To time and mortal custom. – Yet my heart   110
Throbs to know one thing: tell me, – if your art
Can tell so much, – shall Banquo's issue ever
Reign in this kingdom?

ALL   Seek to know no more.

MACBETH I will be satisfied: deny me this,   115
And an eternal curse fall on you! Let me know: –
Why sinks that cauldron? and what noise is this?   *(Hautboys.*

1 WITCH Show!

2 WITCH Show!

3 WITCH Show!   120

ALL Show his eyes and grieve his heart;
Come like shadows, so depart!

Eight Kings *appear, and pass over in order, the last with a glass
in his hand;* BANQUO *following.*

MACBETH Thou art too like the spirit of Banquo; down!
Thy crown does sear mine eye-balls: – and thy hair,
Thou other gold-bound brow, is like the first:–   125
A third is like the former. – Filthy hags!
Why do you show me this? – A fourth? – Start, eyes!
What! will the line stretch out to the crack of doom?

1 the crown

2 Again, the prophecy is
    deceptive, since the
    words seem to suggest
    something which is
    contradicted by the child
    with the tree in his hand.
    Macbeth notes only the
    words "never vanquished",
    which make him feel
    secure.

3 force into service

4 prophecies

5 the allotted span of life

Another yet? – A seventh? – I'll see no more: –
And yet the eighth appears, who bears a glass   130
Which shows me many more; and some I see
That (1) twofold balls and treble sceptres carry:
Horrible sight! – Now, I see, 'tis true;
For the (2) blood-bolter'd Banquo smiles upon me,
And points at them for his. – What! is this so?   135
1 Witch Ay, sir, all this is so: – (3) but why
    Stands Macbeth thus amazedly? –
(4) Come, sisters, cheer we up his sprites,
And show the best of our delights;
I'll charm the air to give a sound,   140
While you perform your antic round;
That this great king may kindly say,
Our duties did his welcome pay.

Music. The Witches *dance, and then vanish.*
Macbeth Where are they? Gone? – Let this pernicious hour
    Stand aye accursed in the calendar! –   145
Come in, without there.

Enter Lennox.
Lennox   What's your grace's will?
Macbeth Saw you the weird sisters?
Lennox   No, my lord.
Macbeth Came they not by you?   150
Lennox   No, indeed, my lord.
Macbeth Infected be the air whereon they ride;
    (5) And damn'd all those that trust them! – I did hear
The galloping of horse: who was't came by?
Lennox 'Tis two or three, my lord, that bring you word   155
    Macduff is fled to England.
Macbeth   Fled to England!
Lennox Ay, my good lord.
Macbeth Time, (6) thou anticipat'st my dread exploits:
The flightly purpose never is o'ertook   160
Unless the deed go with it: from this moment
The very (7) firstlings of my heart shall be
The firstlings of my hand. And even now,
To crown my thoughts with acts, be it thought and done:
The castle of Macduff I will surprise;   165
(8) Seize upon Fife; give to the edge o' the sword

1 reference to the double coronation of James I and VI, in England and Scotland

2 with blood-matted hair

3 a maliciously ironic comment. The Witches' signs have first seemed to offer security, and then undermined that with the prospect that the crown will pass to Banquo's descendants; Macbeth is appalled.

4 The Witches speech is not Shakespearian.

5 A striking irony. He does not realise that he refers to himself.

6 Time, by perceiving what Macbeth intends, has frustrated him in the deed.

7 What I conceive shall immediately be executed. A repetition of his own earlier resolve to act spontaneously first, and think afterwards (Act III, sc. iv, 162).

8 Macbeth's language reveals an obsession with the crown and with inheritance. He embarks now on purposeless and vicious action in revenge against Macduff's family, since he cannot reach the man himself. It is as if in killing Macduff's children he is striking at Banquo's progeny who will inherit the crown.

His wife, his babes and all unfortunate souls
That trace him in his line. No boasting like a fool;
This deed I'll do before this purpose cool:
But no more sights! – Where are these gentlemen?   **170**
Come, bring me where they are.   *Exeunt.*

ACT FOUR, SCENE TWO
FIFE – A ROOM IN MACDUFF'S CASTLE

Enter LADY MACDUFF, *her* SON, *and* ROSS.

LADY MACDUFF What had he done, to make him fly the land?
ROSS You must have patience madam.
LADY MACDUFF He had none:
    His flight was madness: when our actions do not,
    Our fears do make us traitors.   **5**
ROSS   You know not
    Whether it was his wisdom or his fear.
LADY MACDUFF Wisdom! to leave his wife, to leave his babes,
    His mansion, and his titles, in a place
    From whence himself does fly? He loves us not: **10**
    He [1] wants the natural touch; for the poor wren,
    The most diminutive of birds, will fight,
    Her young ones in her nest, against the owl.
    All is the fear, and nothing is the love;
    As little is the wisdom, where the flight   **15**
    So runs against all reason.
ROSS   My dearest coz,
    I pray you, school yourself: but, for your husband,
    He is noble, wise, judicious, and best knows
    The [2] fits o' the season. I dare not speak much further: **20**
    But cruel are the times, when we are traitors,
    And do not know ourselves; when we [3] hold rumour
    From what we fear, yet know not what we fear,
    But float upon a wild and violent sea
    Each way and move. – I take my leave of you: **25**
    Shall not be long but I'll be here again:
    Things at the worst will cease, or else climb upward
    To what they were before. – My pretty cousin,
    Blessing upon you!
LADY MACDUFF Father'd he is, and yet he's fatherless.   **30**

This touching scene dramatises the widespread suspicion and suffering in Scotland under the tyrant's rule, by showing them in Macduff's wife and child. The violent images of cruel death make clear how far Macbeth has deteriorated, the murder of an innocent child being an extreme violation of the most natural of bonds.

1 lacks

2 fluctuating crises of the time

3 when fear makes us believe rumours although we are not even clear what we are afraid of

Ross I am so much a fool, should I stay longer,
　(1) It would be my disgrace and your discomfort:
　I take my leave at once.　　　　　　　　　　　*Exit.*

Lady Macduff　　　　　　Sirrah, your father's dead;
　And what will you do now? How will you live?　　35

Son As (2) birds do, mother.

Lady Macduff　　　　　　What, with worms and flies?

Son With what I get, I mean; and so do they.

Lady Macduff Poor bird! thou'dst never fear the net nor lime,
　(3) The pit-fall nor the gin.　　　　　　　　　40

Son Why should I, mother? Poor birds they are not set for.
　My father is not dead, for all your saying.

Lady Macduff Yes, he is dead: how wilt thou do for a father?

Son Nay, how will you do for a husband?

Lady Macduff Why, I can buy me twenty at any market.　45

Son Then you'll buy 'em to sell again.

Lady Macduff Thou speak'st with all thy wit; and yet, i' faith,
　With wit enough for thee.

Son Was my father a traitor, mother?

Lady Macduff Ay, that he was.　　　　　　　　　50

Son What is a traitor?

Lady Macduff Why, one that swears and lies.

Son And be all traitors that do so?

Lady Macduff Every one that does so is a traitor,
　and must be hanged.　　　　　　　　　　　55

Son And must they all be hanged that swear and lie?

Lady Macduff Every one.

Son Who must hang them?

Lady Macduff Why, the honest men.

Son Then the liars and swearers are fools, (4) for there are liars and　60
　swearers enow to beat the honest men, and hang up them.

Lady Macduff Now, God help thee, poor monkey! But how wilt
　thou do for a father?

Son If he were dead, you'd weep for him. (5) If you would not, it were
　a good sign that I should quickly have a new father.　65

Lady Macduff Poor prattler! how thou talk'st.

　Enter a Messenger.

Messenger Bless you, fair dame! I am not to you known,
　Though in your (6) state of honour I am perfect.
　I doubt some danger does approach you nearly:
　If you will take a homely man's advice,　　　70

1　He would disgrace himself by weeping, and embarrass her.

2　Here natural imagery reinforces the images of unnatural cruelty which follow.

3　These are methods of trapping birds.

4　The little boy's cynical wisdom reflects sadly on the state of the world he sees round him.

5　His natural reactions to his mother's tears makes his impending murder seem yet more unnatural.

6　I am perfectly clear of your rank.

Be not found here; hence, with your little ones.
To fright you thus, methinks, I am too savage;
To do worse to you were fell cruelty,
Which is too nigh your person. Heaven preserve you!
I dare abide no longer.   *Exit.*   **75**

LADY MACDUFF Whither should I fly?
I have done no harm. But I remember now
I am in this earthly world; where to do harm
Is often laudable; to do good, sometime
Accounted dangerous folly: why then, alas,   **80**
Do I put up that womanly defence,
To say I have done no harm? – What are these faces?

Enter Murderers.

1 MURDERER Where is your husband?
LADY MACDUFF I hope, in no place so unsanctified
Where such as thou mayst find him.   **85**
1 MURDERER   He's a traitor.
SON Thou liest, thou shag-hair'd villain.
1 MURDERER   What, you egg? *(Stabbing him.*
Young [1] fry of treachery!
SON   He has kill'd me, mother: **90**
Run away, I pray you!   *(Dies.*
                              Exit LADY MACDUFF, *crying Murder,*
                              and pursued by the Murderers.

ACT FOUR, SCENE THREE
ENGLAND – BEFORE THE KING'S PALACE

Enter MALCOLM, *and* MACDUFF.

MALCOLM [2] Let us seek out some desolate shade, and there
Weep our sad bosoms empty.
MACDUFF   Let us rather
Hold fast the [3] mortal sword, and, like good men,
[4] Bestride our down-fall'n birthdom: each new morn   **5**
New widows howl; new orphans cry; new sorrows
Strike heaven on the face, that it resounds
As if it felt with Scotland, and yell'd out
[5] Like syllable of dolour.
MALCOLM   What I believe, I'll wail;   **10**

1 offspring (as in 'small fry'
today)

2 This static but impressive
scene dramatises, in a
more intense and less
poignant way than the
last, the doubts and
suspicions of Scotland. It
also pertinently analyses
the nature of both
kingship and tyranny.

3 deadly

4 defend by standing
protectively over, as one
would over a fallen leader

5 similar sounds of grief

What know, believe; and what I can [1] redress,
As I shall find the time to friend, I will.
What you have spoke, it may be so perchance.
This tyrant, whose sole name blisters our tongues,
Was once thought honest: you have lov'd him well;   15
[2] He hath not touch'd you yet. I am young; but [3] something
You may deserve of him through me; and wisdom
To offer up a weak, poor, innocent lamb
To appease an angry god.

MACDUFF I am not treacherous.   20

MALCOLM   But Macbeth is.
A good and virtuous nature may recoil
In an [4] imperial charge. But I shall crave your pardon;
That which you are, my thoughts cannot [5] transpose;
Angels are bright still, though the brightest fell: 25
Though all things foul would wear the brows of grace,
Yet grace must still look so.

MACDUFF   I have lost my hopes.

MALCOLM Perchance even there where I did find my doubts.
Why in that [6] rawness left you wife and child, –   30
Those precious motives, those strong knots of love, –
Without leave-taking? – I pray you,
Let not my [7] jealousies be your dishonours,
But mine own safeties: – you may be rightly just,
Whatever I shall think.   35

MACDUFF   Bleed, bleed, poor country!
Great tyranny, lay thou thy basis sure,
For goodness dare not check thee! [8] wear thou thy wrongs,
Thy [9] title is affeer'd. – Fare thee well, lord:
I would not be the villain that thou think'st   40
For the whole space that's in the tyrant's grasp
And the rich East [10] to boot.

MALCOLM   Be not offended:
I speak not as in absolute fear of you.
I think our country sinks beneath [11] the yoke;   45
It weeps, it bleeds; and each new day a gash
Is added to her wounds: I think, withal,
There would be hands uplifted in my right;
And here, from gracious England, have I offer
Of goodly thousands: but, for all this,   50
When I shall tread upon the tyrant's head,
Or wear it on my sword, yet my poor country

1   cure, when I find
    favourable opportunity

2   Dramatic irony. The
    audience knows,
    although neither Macduff
    nor Malcolm is yet aware,
    of the deaths of Macduff's
    family by Macbeth's
    orders.

3   You may be seeking
    reward from him by
    betraying me.

4   in carrying out a
    superior's will

5   alter

6   haste

7   do not let my suspicions,
    product of my fears,
    dishonour you - you *may*
    still be just

8   openly show your
    wickedness

9   the name of tyrant is
    confirmed

10 also

11 the burden of Macbeth's
    misrule

Shall have more vices than it had before;
(1) More suffer, and more sundry ways than ever,
By him that shall succeed.   55
MACDUFF   What should he be?
MALCOLM It is myself I mean: in whom I know
All the particulars of vice so *(2)* grafted
That, when they shall be open'd, black Macbeth
(3) Will seem as pure as snow; and the poor state   60
Esteem him as a lamb, being compar'd
With my *(4)* confineless harms.
MACDUFF   Not in the legions
Of horrid hell can come a devil more damn'd
In evils to top Macbeth.   65
MALCOLM I grant him bloody,
(5) Luxurious, avaricious, false, deceitful,
Sudden, malicious, smacking of every sin
That has a name: but there's no bottom, none,
In my voluptuousness: your wives, your daughters,   70
Your matrons, and your maids, could not fill up
The cistern of my lust; and my desire
All *(6)* continent impediments would o'erbear,
That did oppose my will: better Macbeth
Than such a one to reign.   75
MACDUFF   Boundless intemperance
In nature is a tyranny; it hath been
The untimely emptying of the happy throne,
And fall of many kings. But fear not yet
To take upon you what is yours: you may   80
Convey your pleasures in a spacious plenty,
And yet seem cold, the time you may so hoodwink.
We have willing dames enough; there cannot be
(7) That vulture in you, to devour so many
As will to greatness dedicate themselves,   85
Finding it so inclin'd.
MALCOLM   With this there grows,
In my most ill-compos'd affection, such
A *(8)* stanchless avarice, that, were I king,
I should cut off the nobles for their lands;   90
Desire his jewels, and this other's house:
And my more-having would be as a sauce
To make me hunger more; that I should forge
Quarrels unjust against the good and loyal,

1 Scotland shall suffer
   more, and in a variety of
   different ways, under my
   rule as king.

2 rooted. Malcolm has to
   present a false picture of
   himself to test Macduff's
   integrity and loyalty to
   Scotland; even goodness
   now can only work
   covertly, through guile.

3 The images of snow and
   lamb applied to Macbeth
   are strikingly
   inappropriate.

4 unrestrainable, limitless

5 lustful

6 restraining obstacles

7 Your lust cannot be so
   predatory that it will not
   be satisfied by all the
   women who, since you
   are king, will be willing
   to sacrifice themselves to
   you.

8 unquenchable

Destroying them for wealth.   95
MACDUFF   This avarice
    Sticks deeper; grows with more pernicious root
    Than *(1)* summer-seeming lust; and it hath been
    The sword of our slain kings: yet do not fear;
    Scotland hath *(2)* foysons to fill up your will,   100
    Of your *(3)* mere own: all these are portable,
    With other graces weigh'd.
MALCOLM But I have none: the king-becoming graces,
    As justice, verity, temperance, stableness,
    Bounty, perseverance, mercy, lowliness,   105
    Devotion, patience, courage, fortitude,
    I have no *(4)* relish of them; but abound
    In the division of each several crime,
    Acting it many ways. Nay, had I power, I should
    (5) Pour the sweet milk of concord into hell,   110
    Uproar the universal peace, confound
    All unity on earth.
MACDUFF   O Scotland! Scotland!
MALCOLM If such a one be fit to govern, speak:
    I am as I have spoken.   115
MACDUFF   Fit to govern!
    No, not to live! – O nation miserable,
    With an untitled tyrant bloody-scepter'd,
    When shalt thou see thy wholesome days again,
    Since that the truest issue of thy throne   120
    By his own *(6)* interdiction stands accurs'd,
    And does blaspheme his breed? – Thy royal father
    Was a most sainted king; the queen that bore thee,
    Oftener upon her knees than on her feet,
    Died every day she lived. Fare thee well!   125
    These evils thou repeat'st upon thyself
    Have banish'd me from Scotland. – O my breast,
    Thy hope ends here!
MALCOLM   Macduff, this noble passion,
    Child of intregity, hath from my soul   130
    Wip'd the black *(7)* scruples, reconcil'd my thoughts
    To thy good truth and honour. Devilish Macbeth
    By many of these *(8)* trains hath sought to win me
    Into his power; and modest wisdom plucks me
    From over-credulous haste: but God above   135
    Deal between thee and me! for even now

1 lust that is quickly burnt
out with your youth

2 treasures

3 amongst your
possessions

4 hint, touch

5 A powerful image of
universal discord, which
fittingly describes what
Macbeth has done. The
imagery ironically recalls
Lady Macbeth's
description of her
husband as being 'too full
of the milk of human
kindness'.

6 accusation

7 suspicions

8 intrigues, stratagems

I put myself to thy direction, and
Unspeak mine own detraction; there [1] abjure
The taints and blames I laid upon myself,
For strangers to my nature. I am yet   140
Unknown to woman; never was [2] forsworn,
Scarcely have coveted what was mine own;
At no time broke my faith; would not betray
The devil to his fellow; and delight
No less in truth than life: my first false speaking   145
Was this upon myself: – what I am truly,
Is thine, and my poor country's, to command:
Whither, indeed, before thy here-approach,
Old Siward, with ten thousand warlike men,
Already at a point, was setting forth: 150
Now we'll together; and [3] the chance of goodness
Be like our warranted quarrel! Why are you silent?

MACDUFF Such welcome and unwelcome things at once
'Tis hard to reconcile.

Enter a Doctor

MALCOLM Well; more anon. – Comes the king forth, I pray you?   155
DOCTOR Ay, sir: there are a crew of wretched souls
That stay his cure: their [4] malady convinces
The great assay of art; but, at his touch,
Such sanctity hath Heaven given his hand,
They presently amend.   160
MALCOLM   I thank you, doctor.   *Exit* Doctor.
MACDUFF What's the disease he means?
MALCOLM   'Tis called the evil:
A most miraculous work in this good king;
Which often, since my here-remain in England,   165
I have seen him do. How he solicits heaven,
Himself best knows: but [5] strangely-visited people,
All swoln and ulcerous, pitiful to the eye,
The mere despair of surgery, he cures;
Hanging a golden stamp about their necks,   170
Put on with holy prayers: and 'tis spoken,
To the succeeding royalty he leaves
The healing benediction. With this strange virtue,
He hath a heavenly gift of prophecy;
And sundry blessings hang about his throne,   175
[6] That speak him full of grace.

---

1 deny, forswear

2 a liar

3 may our hopes of success
   be as sure as our cause is
   just

4 their sickness defeats the
   greatest medical skills

5 mysteriously infected

6 This description of
   Edward the Confessor
   could not be a greater
   contrast with Macbeth.
   The healing of bodily ills
   points us ironically to
   Macbeth's desires to find
   remedy for both his wife's
   torment and his
   country's, for which the
   only cure is the re-
   assertion of natural
   justice and the removal
   of Macbeth himself. The
   tyrant *is* the disease; the
   true king cures it.

MACDUFF See, who comes here?

MALCOLM My countryman; but yet I know him not.

Enter ROSS.

MACDUFF My ever-gentle cousin, welcome hither.

MALCOLM I know him now. Good God, betimes remove   180
    The means that makes us strangers!

ROSS Sir, amen.

MACDUFF Stands Scotland where it did?

ROSS Alas, poor country, –
    Almost afraid to know itself! It cannot   185
    Be call'd our mother, but our grave: where *(1)* nothing,
    But who knows nothing, is once seen to smile;
    Where sighs, and groans, and shrieks, that rent the air,
    Are *(2)* made, not mark'd; where violent sorrow seems
    A *(3)* modern ecstacy; the *(4)* dead man's knell   190
    Is there scarce ask'd for who; and good men's lives
    Expire before the flowers in their caps,
    Dying or ere they sicken.

MACDUFF O, *(5)* relation
    Too nice, and yet too true!   195

MALCOLM What's the newest grief?

ROSS *(6)* That of an hour's age doth hiss the speaker;
    Each minute teems a new one.

MACDUFF How does my wife?

ROSS Why, well.   200

MACDUFF And all my children?

ROSS Well too.

MACDUFF The tyrant has not batter'd at their peace?

ROSS No; they were well at peace when I did leave 'em.

MACDUFF Be not a *(7)* niggard of your speech: how goes't?   205

ROSS When I came hither to transport the tidings,
    Which I have heavily borne, there ran a rumour
    Of many worthy fellows that were *(8)* out;
    Which was to my belief witness'd the rather,
    For that I saw the tyrant's power a-foot: 210
    Now is the time of help; your eye in Scotland
    Would create soldiers, make our women fight,
    To doff their dire distresses.

MALCOLM Be't their comfort
    We are coming thither: gracious England hath   215
    Lent us good Siward and ten thousand men;

1 nobody is seen to smile, unless they are totally ignorant

2 hardly even noticed, so commonplace are they

3 a contemporary excitement

4 people no longer ask for whom the bell tolls

5 account too explicit

6 a grief an hour old may be scorned as out-of-date news

7 a miser with your words

8 ready to fight Macbeth, of which I had definite proof

An older and a better soldier none
That Christendom gives out.

ROSS   'Would I could answer
This comfort with the like! But I have words   220
That would be howl'd out in the desert air,
Where hearing should not [1] latch them.

MACDUFF What concern they?
The general cause? or is it a [2] fee-grief
Due to some single breast?   225

ROSS   No mind that's honest
But in it shares some woe; though the main part
Pertains to you alone.

MACDUFF   If it be mine,
Keep it not from me; quickly let me have it.   230

ROSS Let not your ears despise my tongue for ever,
Which shall possess them with the heaviest sound
That ever yet they heard.

MACDUFF   Hum! I guess at it.

ROSS Your castle is surpris'd; your wife and babes   235
Savagely slaughter'd: to relate the manner,
Were, on the [3] quarry of these murder'd deer,
To add the death of you.

MALCOLM   Merciful heaven! –
What, man! [4] ne'er pull your hat upon your brows: 240
Give sorrow words: the grief that does not speak
Whispers the [5] o'er-fraught heart, and bids it break.

MACDUFF My children too?

ROSS   Wife, children, servants, all
That could be found.   245

MACDUFF   And I must be from thence!
My wife kill'd too?

ROSS   I have said.

MALCOLM   Be comforted:
Let's make us medicines of our great revenge,   250
To cure this deadly grief.

MACDUFF [6] He has no children. – All my pretty ones?
Did you say all? – O hell-kite! – All?
What, all my pretty chickens and their dam
At one fell swoop?   255

MALCOLM   Dispute it like a man.

MACDUFF I shall do so;
But I must also feel it as a man:

1   which should be howled
    out in a remote desert,
    where hearing could not
    pick them out

2   a private sorrow

3   a heap of prey (Lady
    Macduff and the children
    are likened to the corpses
    left after a day's hunting)

4   do not hide your grief
    away

5   over-stressed

6   Either 1) Macbeth has no
    children, or he could not
    have done the deed, or 2)
    Malcolm has no children

I cannot but remember such things were,
That were most precious to me. – Did heaven look on,   260
And would not take their part? Sinful Macduff,
(1) They were all struck for thee! naught that I am,
Not for their own demerits, but for mine,
Fell slaughter on their souls: heaven rest them now!

MALCOLM Be this the whetstone of your sword; let grief   265
Convert to anger; blunt not the heart, enrage it.

MACDUFF O, I could (2) play the woman with mine eye,
And braggart with my tongue! – But, gentle heavens,
Cut short all intermission; front to front
Bring thou this fiend of Scotland and myself;   270
Within my sword's length set him; if he 'scape,
Heaven forgive him too!

MALCOLM   This tune goes manly.
Come, go we to the king; our power is ready;
Our (3) lack is nothing but our leave: Macbeth   275
Is ripe for shaking, and the powers above
Put on their instruments. Receive what cheer you may;
The night is long that never finds the day.   *Exeunt.*

*1 it was for my faults,
worthless as I am, that
they were all killed*

*2 I could weep like a
woman, and rant, but ...*

*3 all we must do now is
depart*

ACT FIVE, (4) SCENE ONE

DUNSINANE – A ROOM IN THE CASTLE

Enter a Doctor of Physic *and a* Waiting-Gentlewoman.

DOCTOR I have two nights watched with you, but can perceive no truth
in your report. When was it she last walked?

GENTLEWOMAN Since his majesty went into the field, I have seen her
rise from her bed, throw her nightgown upon her, unlock her
closet, take forth paper, fold it, write upon it, read it, after-wards   5
seal it, and again return to bed; yet all this while in a
most fast sleep.

DOCTOR A great (5) perturbation in nature, – to receive at once the benefit
of sleep, and do the effects of watching! – In this slumbery
agitation, besides her walking and other actual performances,   10
what, at any time, have you heard her say?

GENTLEWOMAN That, sir, which I will not report after her.

DOCTOR You may to me; and 'tis most meet you should.

*4 This is the only scene
other than the brief
interlude with the Porter,
that is wholly in prose.
The use of prose shocks
us by suggesting a
normal everyday
experience, when the
action is abnormal and
unnatural in the extreme.*

5 disturbance

GENTLEWOMAN [1] Neither to you nor any one; having no witness to
confirm my speech. Lo you, here she comes!   15

Enter LADY MACBETH, *with a taper.*
This is her [2] very guise; and, upon my life, fast asleep.
Observe her; stand close.

DOCTOR How came she by the light?

GENTLEWOMAN Why, it stood by her: she has light by her continually;
'tis her command.   20

DOCTOR You see, her eyes are open.

GENTLEWOMAN Ay, but their sense is shut.

DOCTOR What is it she does now? Look, how she rubs her hands.

GENTLEWOMAN It is an accustomed action with her, to seem thus
washing her hands: I have known her continue in this a quarter of   25
an hour.

LADY MACBETH Yet here's a spot.

DOCTOR Hark! she speaks: I will set down what comes from her,
to satisfy my remembrance the more strongly.

LADY MACBETH Out, damned spot! out, I say! – One; two. Why, then 'tis   30
time to do't: – Hell is murky! – Fie, my [3] lord, fie! a soldier, and
afeard? What need we fear who knows it, when none can call our
power to account? Yet who would have thought the old man to
have had so much blood in him?

DOCTOR Do you mark that?   35

LADY MACBETH The Thane of Fife had a wife; where is she now? – What,
will these hands ne'er be clean? – No more o' that, my lord, no
more o' that: you mar all with this starting.

DOCTOR Go to, go to; you have known what you should not.

GENTLEWOMAN She has spoke what she should not, I am sure of that: 40
heaven knows what she has known.

LADY MACBETH Here's the smell of the blood still: all the perfumes of
Arabia will not sweeten this little hand. Oh, oh, oh!

DOCTOR What a sigh is there! The heart is sorely charged.

GENTLEWOMAN I would not have such a heart in my bosom for the   45
[4] dignity of the whole body.

DOCTOR Well, well, well, –

GENTLEWOMAN Pray God it be, sir.

DOCTOR This disease is beyond my practice: yet I have known those
which have walked in their sleep who have died holily in their   50
beds.

---

1 what looks at first like
   loyalty to Lady Macbeth
   in the Gentlewoman's
   speech is shown to be
   suspicious caution

2 her usual practice

3 Lady Macbeth rehearses
   again the most
   unforgettable moments
   of crisis for her and her
   husband: his and her own
   fear, her own guilt, the
   deaths of Lady Macduff
   and Banquo, and the
   knocking at the gate after
   Duncan's murder. In
   dream, she is again
   trying to control
   Macbeth's frantic fear and
   guilt. Her absolute
   devotion to him is tragic.

4 however royal my body

LADY MACBETH Wash your hands, put on your nightgown; look not so
    pale: – I tell you yet again, Banquo's buried; he cannot come out
    on's grave.   55

DOCTOR Even so?

LADY MACBETH To bed, to bed; there's knocking at the gate: come,
    come, come, come, give me your hand: what's done cannot be
    undone: to bed, to bed, to bed.   *Exit.*

DOCTOR Will she go now to bed?   60

GENTLEWOMAN Directly.

DOCTOR Foul whisperings are abroad: unnatural deeds
    Do breed unnatural troubles: infected minds
    To their deaf pillows will discharge their secrets.
    More needs she the divine than the physician. –   65
    God, God, forgive us all! – Look after her;
    Remove from her the means of all [1] annoyance,   *1 harm*
    And still keep eyes upon her: – so, good-night:
    My mind she has [2] mated, and amaz'd my sight: *2 astounded*
    I think, but dare not speak.   70

GENTLEWOMAN Good-night, good doctor.   *Exeunt.*

ACT FIVE, SCENE TWO

THE COUNTRY NEAR DUNSINANE

Enter with drum and colours, MENTEITH, CAITHNESS, ANGUS, LENNOX
and Soldiers.

MENTEITH The English power is near, led on by Malcolm,
    His uncle Siward, and the good Macduff.
    Revenges burn in them; for their dear causes
    Would [3] to the bleeding and the grim alarm   *3 would raise even the dead*
    Excite the mortified man.   5   *to the blood and violence*

ANGUS   Near Birnam wood   *of war*
    Shall we well meet them; that way are they coming.

CAITHNESS Who knows if Donalbain be with his brother?

LENNOX For certain, sir, he is not: I have a file
    Of all the gentry: there is Siward's son,   10
    And many [4] unrough youths, that even now   *4 newly-shaven*
    [5] Protest their first of manhood.   *5 witness that they have*

MENTEITH   What does the tyrant?   *newly reached manhood*

CAITHNESS Great Dunsinane he strongly fortifies:
    Some say he's mad; others, that lesser hate him,   15

Do call it valiant fury: but, for certain,
(1) He cannot buckle his distemper'd cause
Within the belt of rule.

ANGUS   Now does he feel
His secret murders sticking on his hands;   20
Now (2) minutely revolts upbraid his faith-breach;
Those he commands move only in command,
Nothing in love: now does he feel his title
(3) Hang loose about him, like a giant's robe
Upon a dwarfish thief.   25

MENTEITH   Who, then, shall blame
His (4) pester'd senses to recoil and start,
When all that is within him does condemn
Itself for being there?

CAITHNESS   Well, march we on,   30
To give obedience where 'tis truly ow'd:
Meet we the medicine of the sickly weal;
(5) And with him pour we, in our country's purge,
Each drop of us.

LENNOX   Or so much as it needs,   35
To dew the sovereign flower, and drown the weeds.
Make we our march towards Birnam.   *Exeunt, marching.*

ACT FIVE, SCENE THREE

DUNSINANE — A ROOM IN THE CASTLE

Enter MACBETH, Doctor *and* Attendants.

MACBETH Bring me no more reports; let them fly all:
(6) Till Birnam wood remove to Dunsinane
I cannot taint with fear. What's the boy Malcolm?
Was he not born of woman? The spirits that know
All mortal consequences have pronounc'd me thus, –   5
Fear not, Macbeth; no man that's born of woman
Shall e'er have power upon thee. – Then fly, false thanes,
And mingle with the English epicures:
The mind I sway by, and the heart I bear.
Shall never sag with doubt nor shake with fear.   10

Enter a Servant.
The devil damn thee black, thou cream-fac'd loon!

1 he lacks the authority to control those who follow his depraved cause
2 each minute brings new rebellion against his tyranny and treachery
3 a marvellous image to suggest Macbeth has dwindled from king to tyrant (if he ever had the dignity and stature of a king). It recalls Banquo's metaphor of 'strange garments' in Act I, sc iii, and Macduff's Lest our old robes sit easier than our new' (Act II, sc. iv, 48) as well as linking with lines 18-19 of this scene. The complex of images suggests deception and pretence.
4 his bewildered senses for recoiling in terror when he is reduced to a constant state of self-condemnation.
5 With Malcolm, let us offer our blood as a violent cure for our infected country. There are several images of curing and purging in this section of the play, as well as the figures of the Doctor who cannot prescribe for a 'mind diseased', and the English king who offers his people 'healing benediction'.
6 Macbeth's confidence in the Witches was never more ironic. As the English move to Birnam, he puts his trust in the prophecy, and assumes that 'to know all mortal consequences' is therefore to be honest about them. His courage is quite spurious.

<u>Where gott'st thou that goose look?</u>

SERVANT There is ten thousand –

MACBETH   Geese, villain?

SERVANT   Soldiers, sir.   15

MACBETH Go, *(1)* <u>prick thy face, and over-red thy fear,</u>

   Thou *(2)* <u>lily-liver'd boy.</u> What soldiers, patch?

   <u>Death of thy soul! those linen cheeks of thine</u>

   <u>Are counsellors to fear.</u> What soldiers, whey-face?

SERVANT The English force, so please you.   20

MACBETH Take thy face hence. Seyton! – I am sick at heart,

                              Exit Servant.

   When I behold – Seyton, I say! – This push

   (3) <u>Will chair me ever</u>, or disseat me now.

   I have liv'd long enough: my way of life

   Is fall'n into the *(4)* sear, the yellow leaf;   25

   And *(5)* <u>that which should accompany old age,</u>

   <u>As honour, love, obedience, troops of friends,</u>

   <u>I must not look to have;</u> but, in their stead,

   Curses not loud but deep, mouth-honour, breath,

   Which the poor heart would fain deny, and dare not.   30

   Seyton! –

   Enter SEYTON

SEYTON What's your gracious pleasure?

MACBETH   What news more?

SEYTON All is confirm'd, my lord, which was reported.

MACBETH <u>I'll fight till from my bones my flesh be hack'd.</u>

   Give me my armour.   35

SEYTON   'Tis not needed yet.

MACBETH I'll put it on.

   Send out more horses, skirr the country round;

   <u>Hang those that talk of fear. – Give me mine armour. –</u>

   How does your patient, doctor?   40

DOCTOR   Not so sick, my lord,

   As she is troubled with thick-coming fancies;

   That keep her from her rest.

MACBETH   Cure her of that:

   (6) Canst thou not minister to a mind diseas'd;   45

   Pluck from the memory a rooted sorrow;

   Raze out the written troubles of the brain;

   And with some sweet oblivious antidote

   Cleanse the stuff'd bosom of that perilous stuff

1   Macbeth's courage is shaken by the white-faced terror of his servant, whom he tells to redden his face with his own blood.

2   The liver was said to be the origin of the passions; hence a white liver was a symptom of cowardice.

3   chair/cheer/disseat. <u>The pun reveals Macbeth's poor remnant of ambition;</u> he still fights to secure his throne (chair) but begins to feel that he may be ousted (disseat) by the impending encounter, which will decide the issue once and for all.

4   withered

5   <u>Macbeth had seen his future in terms of a king, growing old with the respect and love of his court, like Duncan. In a bitter moment he realises fully what he has in place of these hopes.</u>

6   He asks the Doctor to prescribe for his wife's troubles, and erase the torments in her mind. Ironically, the lines apply also to himself, a fact which he half realises. The Doctor's reply makes clear the issue of personal responsibility.

Which weighs upon the heart?   50
DOCTOR   Therein the patient
    Must minister to himself.
MACBETH Throw physic to the dogs, – I'll none of it. –
    <u>Come, put mine armour on; give me my staff:</u> –
    Seyton, send out. – Doctor, the thanes fly from me. –   55
    Come, sir, despatch. – If thou couldst, doctor, *(1)* cast
    The water of my land, find her disease,
    And purge it to a sound and pristine health,
    I would applaud thee to the very echo,
    That should applaud again. – Pull't off, I say. –   60
    What rhubarb, senna, or what purgative drug,
    Would scour these English hence? Hear'st thou of them?
DOCTOR Ay, my good lord; your royal preparation
    Make us hear something.
MACBETH   Bring it after me. –   65
    <u>I will not be afraid of death and *(2)* bane,</u>
    <u>Till Birnam forest come to Dunsinane.</u>
                    Exeunt all except Doctor.
DOCTOR Were I from Dunsinane away and clear,
    Profit again should hardly draw me here.   *Exit.*

1 diagnose

2 harm, destruction

ACT FIVE, SCENE FOUR
COUNTRY NEAR DUNSINANE: A WOOD IN VIEW

Enter with drum and colours, MALCOLM, *old* SIWARD *and his* Son,
MACDUFF, MENTEITH, CAITHNESS, ANGUS, LENNOX, ROSS, *and* SOLDIERS,
marching.

MALCOLM Cousins, I hope the days are near at hand
    That chambers will be safe.
MENTEITH   We doubt it nothing.
SIWARD What wood is this before us?
MENTEITH   The wood of Birnam.   5
MALCOLM Let every soldier hew him down a bough,
    And bear't before him; <u>thereby shall we *(3)* shadow</u>
    <u>The numbers of our host, and make *(4)* discovery</u>
    <u>Err in report of us.</u>
SOLDIER   It shall be done.   10
SIWARD We learn no other but <u>the confident tyrant</u>
    Keeps still in Dunsinane, and will *(5)* endure

3 <u>cause confusion about</u>
   <u>Even here, deception is</u>
   <u>still employed</u>

4 the reports of the
   enemy's spies

5 withstand our siege

Our setting down before't.

MALCOLM   'Tis his main hope:

For where there is advantage to be given,   15

Both more and less have given him the revolt;

And none serve with him but constrained things,

Whose hearts are absent too.

MACDUFF   Let our just censures

Attend the true (1) event, and (2) put we on   20

Industrious soldiership.

SIWARD   The time approaches,

That will with due decision make us know

(3) What we shall say we have, and what we owe.

(4) Thoughts speculative their unsure hopes relate;   25

But certain issue strokes must arbitrate:

Towards which advance the war.

                          Exeunt, marching.

1   outcome

2   let us prepare ourselves for serious hostilities

3   what we have won, and what lost

4   imagined actions can only offer uncertain hopes; actual fighting must decide the outcome

ACT FIVE, SCENE FIVE

DUNSINANE — WITHIN THE CASTLE

Enter, with drum and colours, MACBETH, SEYTON, *and* Soldiers.

MACBETH Hang out our banners on the outward walls;

The cry is still, *They come:* our castle's strength

Will laugh a siege to scorn: here let them lie

Till famine and the ague eat them up:

Were they not (5) forc'd with those that should be ours,   5

We might have met them dareful, beard to beard,

And beat them backward home.

                   (A cry of women within.

What is that noise?

SEYTON It is the cry of women, my good lord.   *Exit.*

MACBETH I have almost forgot the taste of fears: 10

The time has been, my senses would have cool'd

To hear a night-shriek; and (6) my fell of hair

Would at a dismal (7) treatise rouse and stir

As life were in't: I have supp'd full with horrors;

Direness, familiar to my slaught'rous thoughts,   15

Cannot once start me.

5   re-inforced

6   my scalp would creep and my hair rise as if it had life of its own

7   story - <u>accustomed to evil as he is, Macbeth's reactions are now totally unnatural; he cannot respond as he did, for example, when the thought of murder made his hair stand on end</u> (Act I, sc. iii, 144)

Re-enter SEYTON
Wherefore was that cry?
SEYTON The queen, my lord, is dead.
MACBETH She should have died [1] hereafter;
    There would have been a time for [2] such a word. –   20
    [3] To-morrow, and to-morrow, and to-morrow,
    Creeps in this petty pace from day to day,
    To the last syllable of recorded time;
    And all our yesterdays have lighted fools
    The way to dusty death. Out, out, brief candle!   25
    Life's but a walking shadow; a poor player,
    That struts and frets his hour upon the stage,
    And then is heard no more: it is a tale
    Told by an idiot, full of sound and fury,
    Signifying nothing.   30

Enter a Messenger
    Thou com'st to use thy tongue; thy story quickly.
MESSENGER Gracious my lord,
    I should report that which I say I saw,
    But know not how to do it.
MACBETH   Well, say, sir.   35
MESSENGER As I did stand my watch upon the hill,
    I look'd toward Birnam, and anon, methought,
    The wood began to move.
MACBETH   Liar, and slave!   *(Striking him.*
MESSENGER Let me endure your wrath, if't be not so.   40
    Within this three mile may you see it coming;
    I say, a moving grove.
MACBETH   If thou speak'st false,
    Upon the next tree shalt thou hang alive,
    Till famine [4] cling thee: if thy speech be [5] sooth,   45
    I care not if thou dost for me as much. –
    [6] I pull in resolution: and begin
    To doubt the equivocation of the fiend
    That lies like truth: *Fear not, till Birnam wood*
    Do come to Dunsinane: – and now a wood –   50
    Comes toward Dunsinane. – Arm, arm, and out! –
    If this which he [7] avouches does appear,
    There is nor flying hence nor tarrying here.
    I 'gin to be a-weary of the sun,
    And wish the estate o' the world were now undone. –   55

Side notes:

1 at a more fitting time

2 death (and its mourning implications)

3 The repetition of 'tomorrow' not only makes us feel the doleful routine of endless joyless episodes, but intensifies the contrast between vain hopes for the future (such as Macbeth had) and the disillusionment of past actions (yesterdays). Macbeth's ambition ends here.

4 reduce you to skeletal shreds

5 truthful

6 I rein in, restrain

7 swears

Ring the alarum-bell! – Blow, wind! come, *(1)* wrack!
At least we'll die with harness on our back.   *Exeunt.*

ACT FIVE, SCENE SIX
THE SAME. A PLAIN BEFORE THE CASTLE

Enter with drum and colours, MALCOLM, *old* SIWARD, MACDUFF,
etc., and their Army, *with boughs.*

MALCOLM Now near enough; your leafy screens throw down,
(2) And show like those you are. – You, worthy uncle,
Shall, with my cousin, your right-noble son,
Lead our first battle: worthy Macduff and we
Shall take upon's what else remains to do,   5
According to our order.
SIWARD   Fare you well. –
Do we but find the tyrant's power to-night,
Let us be beaten, if we cannot fight.
MACDUFF Make all our trumpets speak; give them all breath,   10
Those clamorous *(3)* harbingers of blood and death.   *Exeunt.*

ACT FIVE, SCENE SEVEN
THE SAME. ANOTHER PART OF THE PLAIN

Alarums – Enter MACBETH.

MACBETH They have tied me to a stake: I can not fly,
But, bear-like, I must fight the *(4)* course. – What's he
That was not born of woman? Such a one
Am I to fear, or none.

Enter young SIWARD
YOUNG SIWARD What is thy name?   5
MACBETH   Thou'lt be afraid to hear it.
YOUNG SIWARD No; though thou call'st thyself a hotter name
Than any is in hell.
MACBETH   My name's Macbeth.
YOUNG SIWARD The devil himself could not pronounce a title   10
More hateful to mine ear.
MACBETH   No, nor more fearful.

1 wreck, destruction.
   Macbeth summons his
   courage despite
   realisation that the
   Witches have 'lied' to
   him and prepares to die
   in battle, so recreating
   our first image of him as
   a valiant soldier. By
   leaving the safety of the
   castle, he lays himself
   open to attack and single
   combat with Macduff,
   and so fulfils the
   prophecy.

2 Part of Macbeth's
   realisation of the truth
   comes from perceiving
   the ease with which he
   has been deceived; here
   the apparent
   impossibility of Birnam
   wood being on the move
   is shown to be a simple
   strategic trick.

3 messengers, prophets

4 like a threatened bear, I
   must face the attack (of
   the dogs, in bear-baiting)

YOUNG SIWARD Thou liest, abhorred tyrant; with my sword
    I'll prove the lie thou speak'st
                (They fight, and young SIWARD *is slain.*

MACBETH Thou wast born of woman. –   15
    (1) But swords I smile at, weapons laugh to scorn,
    Brandish'd by man that's of a woman born.   *Exit.*

    Alarums. Enter MACDUFF.
MACDUFF That way the noise is. – Tyrant, show thy face!
    If thou be'st slain, and with no stroke of mine,
    My wife and children's ghosts will haunt me still.   20
    I cannot strike at wretched *(2)* kerns, whose arms
    Are hir'd to bear their staves; either *(3)* thou, Macbeth,
    Or else my sword, with an unbatter'd edge,
    I sheathe again undeeded. There thou shouldst be;
    By this great clatter, one of greatest note   25
    Seems *(4)* bruited. Let me find him, fortune!
    And more I beg not.   *Exit. Alarums.*

    Enter MALCOLM *and old* SIWARD.
SIWARD This way, my lord; – the castle's gently *(5)* render'd:
    The tyrant's people on both sides do fight;
    The noble thanes do bravely in the war;   30
    The day almost itself professes yours,
    And little is to do.
MALCOLM   We have met with foes
    That strike beside us.
SIWARD   Enter, sir, the castle.   *Exeunt. Alarums.*   35

ACT FIVE, SCENE EIGHT
THE SAME – ANOTHER PART OF THE PLAIN

    Enter MACBETH.

MACBETH Why should I play the *(6)* Roman fool, and die
    On mine own sword? whiles I see lives, the gashes
    Do better upon them.

    Enter MACDUFF.
MACDUFF Turn, hell-hound, turn.
MACBETH Of all men else I have avoided thee.   5

---

1   Still Macbeth persists in his ironic reliance on the Apparition's prophecy, despite the fact that the earlier comment has proved false.

2   puny paid troops

3   either you and I fight in single combat

4   announced, indicated

5   surrendered easily

6   Macbeth refers to the Roman custom whereby a defeated leader in battle would take his own life rather than endure humiliation.

But get thee back; [1] <u>my soul is too much charg'd</u>
<u>With blood of thine already.</u>
MACDUFF   I have no words, –
My voice is in my sword: thou bloodier villain
Than terms can give thee out!   *(They fight.*   10
MACBETH Thou [2] losest labour:
As easy mayst thou the [3] intrenchant air
With thy keen sword impress, as make me bleed:
Let fall thy blade on vulnerable crests;
I bear a charmed life, which must not yield   15
To one of woman born.
MACDUFF   Despair thy charm;
And let the angel whom thou still hast serv'd
Tell thee, Macduff was from his mother's womb
[4] Untimely ripp'd.   20
MACBETH Accursed be that tongue that tells me so,
<u>For it hath cow'd [5] my better part of man!</u>
<u>And be these juggling fiends no more believ'd,</u>
<u>That palter with us in a double sense;</u>
<u>That keep the word of promise to our ear,</u>   25
<u>And break it to our hope!</u> – I'll not fight with thee.
MACDUFF Then yield thee, coward,
And live to be the show and [6] gaze o' the time:
We'll have thee, as our rarer monsters are,
Painted upon a pole, and underwrit,   30
Here may you see the tyrant.
MACBETH <u>I will not yield,</u>
<u>To kiss the ground before young Malcolm's feet,</u>
<u>And to be baited with the rabble's curse.</u>
<u>Though Birnam wood be come to Dunsinane,</u>   35
<u>And thou oppos'd, being of no woman born;</u>
<u>Yet I will try the last. Before my body</u>
<u>I throw my warlike shield: lay on, Macduff;</u>
<u>[7] And damn'd be him that first cries, *Hold, enough!*</u>
                              Exeunt, fighting.

1 An unexpected
   acknowledgement of
   guilt

2 you lose ground
3 invulnerable,
   impenetrable

4 Macbeth's last comfort is
   ironically exploded, and
   Macduff's sarcasm 'the
   angel whom thou still
   hast served' very quickly
   provokes Macbeth's
   attack on the 'juggling
   fiends'.

5 my courage
6 public sensation

7 Macbeth's courage is
   ironic, since whoever
   asks for mercy,
   damnation is in store for
   him.

ACT FIVE, SCENE NINE
WITHIN THE CASTLE

Retreat. Flourish. Enter, with drum and colours, MALCOLM, *old*
SIWARD, ROSS, LENNOX, ANGUS, CAITHNESS, MENTEITH *and* Soldiers.

MALCOLM I would the friends we miss were safe arriv'd.		
SIWARD Some must [1] go off; and yet, by these I see,	5	*1* be killed, die
So great a day as this is cheaply bought.		
MALCOLM Macduff is missing, and your noble son.		
ROSS [2] Your son, my lord, has paid a soldier's debt:		*2* An epitaph which could
He only liv'd but till he was a man;		have been a fulfilment of
The which no sooner had his prowess confirm'd	10	Macbeth's earlier
In the unshrinking station where he fought,		promise, had he not been
But like a man he died.		misled.
SIWARD Then he is dead?		
ROSS Ay, and brought off the field: your cause of sorrow		
Must not be measur'd by his worth, for then	15	
It hath no end.		
SIWARD [3] Had he his hurts before?		*3* Was he wounded while
ROSS Ay, on the front.		facing attack, rather than
SIWARD Why, then, God's soldier be he!		in flight?
Had I as many sons as I have hairs,	20	
I would not wish them to a fairer death:		
And, so his knell is knoll'd.		
MALCOLM He's worth more sorrow,		
And that I'll spend for him.		
SIWARD He's worth no more:	25	
They say he parted well, and [4] paid his score:		*4* paid his debts as he left
And so, God be with him! – Here comes newer comfort.		(like an honest man
		leaving an inn)

Re-enter MACDUFF, *with* MACBETH'S *head.*

MACDUFF Hail, king! for so thou art: behold, where stands		
The usurper's cursed head: the [5] time is free:		*5* the age is now liberated
I see thee compass'd with [6] thy kingdom's pearl	30	*6* surrounded by the most
That speak my salutation in their minds;		precious noblemen of
Whose voices I desire aloud with mine, –		your country
Hail, King of Scotland!		
ALL Hail, King of Scotland! *(Flourish.*		
MALCOLM We shall not spend a large expense of time	35	*7* the loves of each
Before we reckon with [7] your several loves,		individual
And [8] make us even with you. My thanes and kinsmen,		*8* reward you

Henceforth be earls, the [1] first that ever Scotland
In such an honour nam'd. What's more to do,
Which would be planted newly with the time, –   **40**
As calling home our exil'd friends abroad,
That fled the snares of watchful tyranny;
[2] Producing forth the cruel ministers
Of this dead butcher, and his fiend-like queen,
Who, as 'tis thought, by self and violent hands   **45**
[3] Took off her life; – this, and what needful else
That calls upon us, by the grace of Grace,
We will perform in measure, time, and place:
So, thanks to all at once, and to each one,
[4] Whom we invite to see us crown'd at Scone.   **50**

(Flourish. Exeunt.

1 the first ever granted that
   title in Scotland

2 hunting up for justice

3 with her own violent
   hands ended her life

4 So the coronation of the
   new righteous king, and
   his royal rituals of
   thanks, reward and just
   punishment establish a
   sense of the revived
   stability and harmony of
   the realm. It also recalls
   the dignified court of
   Duncan, which Macbeth
   destroyed.